'Martyn Pig' by Kevin Brooks: the Student Study Guide

Natalie Twigg

and

David Wheeler

ISBN: 978-1505286694

Contents

The Author

Kevin Brooks was born on March 30th 1959 near Exeter in Devon and spent many years doing a wide variety of jobs while trying to find success as a writer. *Martyn Pig* was his first novel to be published (on April 1st, 2002 by The Chicken House) and received immediate praise and acclaim. It was awarded the Branford Boase Award in 2003 and was on the short list for the 2002 Carnegie Prize. *The School Library Journal* wrote of *Martyn Pig*: 'Gripping plot twists... fresh and edgy... will have tremendous teen appeal'. While *Novellist* in its review of the novel commented: 'A breathless read... the macabre details are as compelling as the edgy realism'. In the USA it was chosen as a *Publishers' Weekly* Flying Start and an American Library Association Novel of the Year. Since the publication and success of *Martyn Pig*, Brooks has become a full-time writer and has become famous for novels aimed at the teen and young adult market. He specializes in unusual and bizarre plots combined with the edgy realism that characterizes *Martyn Pig*. Interestingly all his novels so far have used a teenager, a character in the story, as the first person narrator. This is an important stylistic feature which has important implications for the way the plot is told, the reader's sympathy and empathy for the narrator – and the revelation of parts of the plot that the narrator is unaware of. This issue is discussed fully later in this guide. Certainly

Brooks feels, as revealed in interviews, that the adoption of a character's voice and point of view, allows him to tell the story from that character's unique perspective, to get inside their head and to write in a voice that is authentic. As we will see in the course of this guide, using Martyn to narrate his own story has important effects on the ways in which the reader reacts to the story and it has a vital impact on the novel's themes and preoccupations.

Plot Summary

In the first chapter 'Wednesday' we are given an extensive introduction to the eponymous narrator's rather miserable life. We are also introduced to Martyn's only friend, Alex, and her obnoxious boyfriend Dean. It is a week before Christmas and Martyn is sent shopping by his bullying father; on his way home he bumps into Alex at the bus stop. That evening Martyn and his father have an argument, caused by Martyn's drunken father loudly mocking a television show that Martyn wanted to watch. Martyn's father tries to hit Martyn, but Martyn dodges the blow and shoves his father. Martyn's father falls, hits his head on the fireplace wall and dies. Martyn's reaction is to do nothing: he does not call the emergency services and the longer he leaves it, the more concerned he becomes that his actions, or rather his lack of action, might make him look guilty in the eyes of the police and the accident of his father's death might look like murder. Alex calls round (as she does most evenings we are told) and tries to convince Martyn to contact the police: he refuses.

In the second chapter, 'Thursday', Martyn opens a letter addressed to his Dad which reveals that he has been left £30,000 by a distant aunt in Australia. Alex calls round, still intent on getting Martyn to contact the police. Martyn, however, argues that his delay in contacting them about his Dad's death will now look even more suspicious and that he will lose all chance of receiving the £30,000. There is the added complication that on the next day Martyn's Aunty Jean will be visiting, expecting to see her brother, Martyn's Dad. Martyn outlines a plan to dump his father's body on the other side of town in a quarry – but he needs Alex to do this, because she is old enough to drive and has access to her mother's car – once it has been repaired. Alex leaves, but returns unexpectedly early, along with her boyfriend, Dean. Dean has put a microphone in Alex's bag and recorded the conversation that she had earlier with Martyn about the money and about their plans to dispose of Martyn's father's body. Dean threatens Martyn with going to the police with the tape recording, unless Martyn gives him all the money. Before the end of the chapter Alex plans what to do and tells Alex, but does not tell the reader.

In Chapter Three, 'Friday', the chief interest is whether Alex and Martyn can convince Aunty Jean that Dad, her brother, is alive. Under the pretext that he is ill and with the help of some make up applied by Alex and a recording made by Alex pretending to be Dad breathing and groaning, they succeed, and Aunty Jean leaves convinced that her brother is alive.

In Chapter Four, 'Saturday', in the morning, having had a phone call from Alex telling him that she will be able to use her mother's car that evening, Martyn takes a bus and visits the local beach where he sits through a snowstorm and reflects about life. In the evening Alex and Martyn dispose of his Dad's body in the local quarry as planned. They put his body in a sleeping bag, taking care to include some of Dean's hairs and his discarded cigarette butts: the plan is obviously to convince the police that Dean murdered Martyn's father.

Chapter Five, 'Sunday', is a very short reflective chapter. Martyn phones Alex several times, but there is no answer until finally Alex's Mum answers and tells him that she is out, but she does not know where. Finally, later in the evening, Alex herself phones and tells Martyn that she had been out that day with her mother – which Martyn and the reader know is a lie. The chapter ends on this note of deep uncertainty.

'Monday' (Chapter Six) is the day that Dean expects to receive the money in exchange for the recording he made of Martyn and Alex discussing both the disposal of Dad's body and the inherited money. Alex leaves on the bus to go to Dean's flat to remove any copies of the tape that he has made. When Dean arrives, Martyn tells him what he and Alex have done with the body: if Dean takes the tape to the police, Martyn will reveal the location of the body – complete with the planted clues that implicate Dean in Dad's death. Dean leaves, defeated, and Martyn and Alex spend the rest of the day playing Scrabble. Ominously and with no explanation, at the end of the chapter when Alex leaves, Martyn tells us 'That was the last time I ever saw her' (p. 173).

On 'Tuesday' (Chapter Seven) Martyn, expecting Alex to come round, discovers that Alex and her Mum have disappeared: the car has gone and their house looks deserted. He comes to the conclusion that Alex and her mother have stolen his money. Just after this disheartening realization that he has been betrayed, the police arrive and take Martyn to the police station for questioning. Dean has died in a motorbike accident, caused by the fact that his brake lines had been deliberately cut: the police know that Dean has visited Martyn's house and discover in Martyn's bathroom a flannel smeared with brake oil. At the police station Martyn has time to think and realizes that not only has Alex stolen his money, she has also killed Dean by cutting his brake cables and may have planted evidence in Martyn's house which suggests that he was involved in Dean's murder. Alex is a murderer and a thief.

Chapter Eight is 'Christmas Day'. Martyn faces more questioning from the police, but manages to convince them that he is innocent of any involvement in Dean's death. The police also reveal that Martyn's Dad's body has been discovered by police divers: they were tipped off about the location by an anonymous phone call during the night. He is released into the care of his Aunty Jean.

The final chapter is set a year later and is entitled 'Epilogue'. Martyn is living at Aunty Jean's house. He has been questioned further by the police who remain suspicious about him but have no evidence to link him with either the death of his father or the murder of Dean. Martyn has received a letter from Alex who is in California pursuing a career as an actress.

First Thoughts

The edition of the novel that we are using prints prominently on the cover two quotations from page 24: 'Did I hate him? Of course I hated him' and 'But I never meant to kill him'. So even before we open the novel and read a single word of the novel, we know that the narrator kills someone he hates - and we don't have to wait long to find out: Martyn tells us that he accidentally kills his Dad on page 24. This is ironic because Martyn is a self-confessed fan of detective stories and murder mysteries, in which the entire plot revolves around finding out who committed a particular murder. In this sense, *Martyn Pig* is a type of anti-mystery murder story: we know who killed Dad and there is no mystery over who the murderer is – Martyn tells us. What Martyn, with Alex's help, does is to construct a trail of evidence (just as in the best detective stories), a trail of clues which are designed to lead the police to the wrong conclusion – that Dean killed Martyn's father. It is a sort of mystery story in reverse. Under English law Martyn would almost certainly not have been tried for murder and probably not even manslaughter: what happened was an accident and his father's abuse of him is a strong mitigating factor. But it is almost as if Martyn's obsession with murder mysteries leads him to construct an elaborate plot – just for the fun of it – to turn an accident into a murder investigation. It seems almost an intellectual challenge: can he dispose of the body and, as the plot develops, can he successfully frame Dean for the murder? But Martyn is unaware – because Brooks makes him unaware, so that the reader is too – that there is another plot being planned. The other plot is being planned by Alex and her mother, and Martyn only works it out after it has happened. Just as in a detective story Brooks has left very subtle clues about the enigmatic Alex, but these 'clues' only become apparent to the reader in retrospect when we look back at the events of the novel in the full knowledge that Alex is a thief and a murderer.

Interestingly, one of Kevin Brooks' favourite genres is the detective novel and he has said in an interview:

I think my awareness of plot comes from having read a lot of crime fiction. When 'Martyn Pig' came out, the reviewers were saying things like 'well plotted' novel. I found that surprising because I didn't have any idea that I could plot or structure a story. I do plan, but I'm not consciously aware that I'm building a plot that creates good suspense; it comes naturally because I've soaked myself in these sorts of plots.

What suspense and tension there is in the novel is in discovering whether Martyn gets away with what he has done and failing to report the accident immediately, and, of course, whether he succeeds in convincing the police that Dean murdered his father. There are other moments of tension too – such as when Aunty Jean visits the dead Dad and Martyn has to convince her that he is alive – but these are shot through with humour. The morning when Dean comes to collect the money is another moment of high tension. Brooks adds further twists and complications to the plot, because Alex is plotting to double-cross Martyn, and steal the money that his father has inherited – but Martyn has no idea that this is going on. At one point Martyn even wonders whether Alex has framed him for the murders of his father and Dean.

So what we read is a novel full of twists and turns and moments of tension. But because Martyn is the narrator we also have long stretches in which Brooks allows Martyn to convey his attitude to life, with long, often highly critical descriptions of his surroundings and explanations of his philosophy or his feelings about life. These digressions are of interest in themselves and also serve to make Martyn a more sympathetic character and one with whom the reader is more likely to empathize.

Chapter One: Wednesday

The author Kevin Brooks quickly establishes his narrator's character and his tone of voice on the opening page of the novel. Martyn Pig, the eponymous narrator, starts by admitting, 'It's hard to know where to start with this' (p. 7) - which immediately signals to the reader what is going to be a key theme of the novel - why things happen as they do or the complex chain of events that lead to a particular outcome - or to put it in Martyn's words 'how things start'.

Brooks seems to allude on the opening page to a famous novel narrated by a cynical and disillusioned teenager – Holden Caulfield in *The Catcher in the Rye*. Compare this from the opening page of *The Catcher in the Rye* by JD Salinger:

If you really want to hear about it, the first thing you'll probably want to know is where I was born and what my lousy childhood was like, and how my parents were occupied and all before they had me, and all that David Copperfield kind of crap, but I don't feel like going into it, if you want to know the truth.

To Martyn's very similar:

I suppose I could tell you all about where I was born, what it was like when mum was still around, what happened when I was a little kid all that kind of stuff, but it's not really relevant. (p 7).

Although Martyn adds as an afterthought: 'Or may be it is' – relevant, he means. As we learn later Martyn is obsessed with how one small occurrence can spark a chain of events which lead to a particular outcome. Holden in *The Catcher in the Rye* is about the same age as Martyn, but is a New York teenager in the 1950s from a wealthy background. However, they do share a despair and disillusionment with the world, an inherent sadness about the state of the world, and a chatty, digressive style of writing.

Brooks evokes immediate sympathy by quickly drawing attention to his protagonist's unusual name: the unusual spelling of 'Martyn' and, worse than that, his unfortunate surname. It conjures up sympathy because Martyn tells us that he has had to put up with 'the startled looks, the sneers and sniggers, the snorts, the never-ending pig jokes, day in, day out over and over again' (p. 7). This name-calling has obviously wounded him deeply. He says on page 8: 'Words *hurt*. Porky, Piggy, Pig Man, Oink, Bacon, Stinky, Snorter, Porker, Grunt'. He has now learnt to ignore these taunts and claims on page 9 that he's used to it: 'you can get used to just about anything given enough time'. But he goes on to add 'At least I don't get called Porky any more. Well... Not very often', which suggests that he is still sensitive about his physical appearance and still the subject of occasional unpleasant remarks or reactions to it. His reaction to the teasing – 'you can get used to just about anything given enough time' - is a stoical and resigned attitude which Martyn applies several times in the novel when thinking about his unhappy life and to different situations.

We are then introduced to Martyn's Dad who is going to play an important, if unwilling, role in the plot and Martyn has already blamed for his unfortunate surname. Our first impression of Martyn's Dad is not a good one: 'Dad was leaning in the doorway, smoking a cigarette, watching me through bloodshot eyes' (p. 9). He shows his ignorance by mispronouncing 'environment' as 'emviroment' and for his generally antisocial attitude shown when he forbids Martyn from taking all the empty beer bottles to the bottle bank to be recycled. I think Martyn is fair to his father. He writes:

He could have been quite handsome man if it wasn't for the drink. Handsome in a short, thuggish kind of way. Five foot seven, tough-guy mouth, squarish jaw, oily black hair. (p. 9 - 10)

But the reality is that Martyn's Dad is a drunk and has a 'fat little belly, florid skin, yellowed eyes, sagging cheeks and a big fat neck. Old and worn out of forty'. (p.10).

Martyn's dad raises the subject of 'that bloody woman' and her annual Christmas visit. Martyn explains 'that bloody woman' was 'my Aunty

Jean. Dad's older sister. A terrible woman. Think of the worst person you know, then double it, and you'll be halfway to Aunty Jean' (p. 10). Interestingly, despite the lack of love and affection between Martyn and his father, they are united in their loathing of Aunty Jean. This is not a family full of love and affection: Martyn writes that his dad 'detested her. Hated her' (p. 10). The days before her visits are spent hiding all Dad's alcohol in the loft. This is because when Martyn's mother left the family home, Aunty Jean tried to get custody of Martyn: 'she reckons the authorities would decide in her favour once they knew of Dad's wicked drunkard ways. They'd never allow me to live with a boozer' (p. 11). However, Martyn shows his cynicism about Aunty Jean's motives when he says on page 11 'she didn't give a hoot for my innocent life she just wanted to kick Dad while he was down, kick him where it hurts, leave him with nothing. She despised him as much as he despised her' (p. 11). Aunty Jean did not get custody of Martyn because Martyn's Dad stopped drinking for over two months and took great care of his personal appearance. However, Martyn knows that this to not out of a sense of responsibility as a father or any love or affection for Martyn:

His need for me was greater than hers. Without me he was just a drunk. But with me he was a drunk with responsibilities, a drunk with child benefit, a drunk with someone to clear up the sick. (p. 11)

For most people Christmas is a time of family togetherness and a celebration of love and peace to the world, but in Martyn's unloving family:

Christmas meant nothing to us. It was just a couple of weeks off school from me and a good excuse for Dad to drink, not that he ever needed one. There was no festive spirit, no goodwill to all men, no robins, no holly – just cold, rainy days with nothing much to do. (p. 12)

Dad gives Martyn £20 to go into town and do some shopping for Christmas, and Martyn once again shows the essential unhappiness of his life by agreeing: 'if he wanted me to go shopping, I'd go shopping.

It gave me something to do' (p. 13). Brooks uses pathetic fallacy – it is raining – to make Martyn's shopping expedition seem very unpleasant. Because we see everything from Martyn's point of view we see how critical he is of the tawdry, poor quality and ramshackle attempts to get the town centre in the Christmas spirit. His cynical and critical attitude comes out in his description of the Father Christmas outside Sainsbury's who is

The scariest Father Christmas I'd ever seen.... He was so thin and short... stiff black stubble showed on his chin beneath an ill-fitting, off-white Santa beard and – strangest of all, I thought – a pair of brand-new trainers gleamed on his feet. When he Ho-ho-ho'd he sounded like a serial killer. Six plywood reindeer pulled his plywood sleigh. They were painted a shiny chocolate brown, with glittery red eyes and coat-hanger antlers intertwined with plastic holly. (p.13)

Even his memory of meeting Santa as a small child is tainted: 'I can still remember the nasty, scratchy feel of his red nylon trousers, the stickiness of his beard, and a strange fruity smell' (p. 14). The Santa's voice is slurred and he was obviously drunk. In desperation Martyn goes to a shop called the Bargain Bin hoping to find a present for Alex: this is on page 14 and is the first time she is mentioned. While he is in the shop he appears to have an attack of anxiety brought on by the cacophony of noise in the shop. Brooks describes it very vividly so that we can empathize with Martyn's need for silence. All he can hear is:

Horrible tinny Christmas musak blaring out from speakers in the ceiling, synthesised sleigh bells and chirpy pianos, groany old singers trying too hard to be happy – it was unbearable. A great swirling mess of sound searing its way into my head. I tried to ignore it, but it just seemed to get louder and louder.... the sound was paralysing – chattering machine guns, talking animals, wailing police car sirens, dee–dur dee-dur dee-dur, parents shouting at their kids, whacking them on the arm, the kids screaming and crying, the constant beep beep beep of the tills, the music... it was like something out of a nightmare. (p. 14 -15)

We have quoted this at length because the contrast between noise and silence is one that runs throughout the novel. Martyn craves silence which gives him the ability to think and relax and be calm; in the same way, he craves order and tidiness, and reacts badly to the untidiness and general chaos of his home with Dad and, indeed, of the area he lives in. We think this can be related to his general unhappiness and despair: throughout the novel he seems generally to dislike other people *en masse* - either their noisy activities or their sloppy, thoughtless behaviour. However, even outside the shop he is assailed by sounds – 'the constant sound of thousands of people shuffling around the crowded streets, all talking, jabbering away, yammering rubbish to each other' (p. 15).

Martyn's mood as he returns home is very depressed: his arms are aching from the heaviness of the shopping bags and his nose is running: 'Snot dripped from the end of my nose and I had to keep stopping to put down the shopping bags so that I could wipe it' (p. 16). However, his mood brightens when he sees Alex waiting at the bus stop and they have a conversation. Alex is going to be pivotal to the plot of the novel in ways that we cannot predict, but we can say that she is the only character in the novel towards whom Martyn expresses positive and warm emotions: she is his only friend. They know each other well enough for her first remark to Martyn to be, 'Your nose is running' (p. 16). As the conversation continues Brooks reveals their intimacy by the fact that Alex teases Martyn about the pitifully small turkey he has bought ('I think you'll find that's a chicken, Martyn' p. 17) and is mildly flirtatious when she asks if he has bought her a present. Martyn is clearly attracted to Alex, but is fairly reticent about this. He comments:

When she smiled I'd sometimes get this sick feeling in my stomach, like... I don't know what it was like. One of those feelings when you don't know if it's good or if it's bad. One of those (p. 17).

The bus arrives and Alex gets on it, having agreed to go round to Martyn's house at ten that evening – a regular meeting we later discover. As she leaves and Martyn waits hopefully for her to turn and wave, Brooks writes: 'She never looked back' (p. 18). Throughout the rest of the novel, whenever Alex parts from Martyn, she never looks back, and this deserves discussion. It's is an example of prolepsis or proleptic irony which Brooks uses deliberately: the reader only understands the irony in retrospect, when we have read the rest of the novel and found out the truth about Alex. It can also be argued that prolepsis is a very obscure way of hinting at or foreshadowing later events. Certainly as the plot develops and reaches its conclusion, we can look back and say that the fact that she never looked back is symbolic of her lack of genuine feeling for Martyn – but at this stage, of course, we are unaware of this. Not looking back implies not dwelling on the past, looking instead to the future, and also perhaps suggests a lack of real feeling towards Martyn on Alex's part.

Martyn reminisces about how he first came to meet Alex, two years before the novel is set, when Alex and her mum moved into a house just down the road. Martyn makes it clear that he is attracted to her: 'I remember thinking to myself how nice she looked. Nice. She looked nice. Pretty... I liked the way she walked too' (p. 19), but he is also painfully conscious that a romantic relationship with Alex is out of the question – 'she was a young woman, I was just a gawky looking kid. It was a ridiculous idea' (p.19). However, Alex invites Martyn over and his nervousness is apparent: 'walking across the road towards the removal van my legs felt like rubber bands. I'd forgotten how to walk I was wobbling fool. Alex smiled at me and my legs almost gave up' (p. 20). But Alex's affability calms him and they become friends.

Martyn admits to feeling glum (p. 21), mainly because he is jealous of Alex's boyfriend Dean West, who works and has his own motorbike. Martyn is completely dismissive of Dean: 'he rode a motorbike and liked to think he was some kind of biker, but he wasn't. He was just a pale white idiot' (p. 21). Alex recounts bumping into them in Boots the chemists when he was picking up a prescription for his father. What is most interesting is that of Martyn's perception of Alex's attitude to Dean: 'she... looked a bit bored. When she smiled at Dean I could tell she didn't really mean it' (p. 21). Of course, this may be a question of Martyn reassuring himself that she doesn't care very much for her boyfriend, but it might also be seen as another example of prolepsis – Alex can smile without really meaning it. Dean and Alex eventually become aware of Martyn in the chemists, and Dean teases Martyn about his name by calling him 'pig man' and implying that he is in the chemists because he has diarrhea. Again there is another telling detail: Martyn tells us: 'I looked at Alex, hoping for support. She looked away embarrassed' (p. 22). This tiny detail seems of little importance at this point in the novel, but will assume greater significance at the end. Here we can say that she fails to show support for Alex in this minor social encounter during which her boyfriend had teased Martyn: she shows no loyalty to Martyn.

Martyn hesitantly admits to being jealous of Dean, but he argues that the main cause of his irritation is that Alex is simply too nice to have someone like Dean as a boyfriend: 'it was just wrong. All of it. Alex and Dean. Wrong. It stank. It was wrong for her to spend time with him. It was a waste. He was nothing. It was wrong. Wrong. Wrong. Wrong. She was too good for him' (p. 23). As readers, given the way that Brooks presents Dean through Martyn's narration, we think that we are inclined to agree with Martyn on this issue and it raises the question of why Alex is going out with Dean – a question that we discuss later in this book in the character discussion of Alex.

Martyn arrives home and once again pathetic fallacy is used to reflect his mood – the rain was turning to sleet (p. 23) as he arrives home, and in the alleyway to his house he steps over 'dog turds and squashed cigarette ends and bin-liners full of empty beer cans (p. 23). Martyn is still thinking about Alex and Dean and realizes that it has nothing to do with him – 'she can see who she wants' (p. 23) His brutish father questions his lateness, demands his change and issues a veiled threat in case Martyn has forgotten anything. He is also spraying shaving foam on the kitchen windows – a rather ridiculous and stupid attempt to imitate snow, a cheap and futile way of trying to bring some Christmas spirits to the house. Martyn knows better than to antagonize his father and he praises it as a good idea (p. 24).

Martyn's narrative now shifts to build up to the death of his father. The shift occurs in a long paragraph of Martyn's inner monologue which is addressed to the reader and the first sentence of which we have already read on the front cover of the novel:

Did I hate him? He was a drunken slob and he treated me like dirt. What do you think? Of course I hated him. Yeah I hated him. I hated every inch of him. From his broken veins, red-nosed face to his dirty, stinking feet. I hated his beery guts (p.24).

The next sentence, however, stands as a paragraph on its own and is given extra prominence by double spacing: 'But I never meant to kill him' (p. 24), which tells us that Martyn's father will soon die, but that Martyn did not do it intentionally. Now Brooks, having revealed what is about to happen, deliberately delays Dad's death for another twelve pages. We may know that Martyn is going to kill his father (which might be said to reduce the tension at this point), but we have no idea of the circumstances – especially if it is unintentional, so the reader's intrigue and interest is maintained.

Martyn is obsessed with why things happen as they do and how one seemingly trivial incident can have consequences years later. In a long digression he take us all the way back to his tenth or eleventh birthday (he is not sure which). Someone gave him a copy of *The Complete Illustrated Sherlock Holmes*. Initially Martyn was put off by the sheer size of the collection ('nearly 1000 pages' p. 25), but, because he is ill in bed with a virus, his boredom leads him to read it and he reads the whole collection of stories in two days. Then he re-reads it. Martyn Pig is obsessed with detective fiction and crime novels, whether as novels or as television series.

It may be a good idea at this point to point out that Brooks does not present Martyn is a typical teenage boy. In his narrative no mention is made of the music he listens to or any mates that he has; he has no mobile phone and there are no references to any computers in the house. This, of course, stresses the poverty in which Martyn lives, but it is still unusual that he mentions no school friends: Martyn is clearly a very lonely and isolated young man.

Martyn claims with a tortuous logic that is quite amusing that the random gift of the *Complete Illustrated Sherlock Holmes* is what led to his father's death, because it began his obsession with crime novels and later that evening it explains his annoyance with his father, who in a drunken attempt to be amusing, is interrupting and spoiling Martyn's watching of an episode of *Inspector Morse* on the television. So, by Martyn's logic, if that book had not been given to him as a birthday present and if he had not been forced to read it out of boredom because he was stuck in bed with a virus, then his father would still be alive!

However, the moment of his father's death is yet to come. While Martyn unpacks the shopping, does the washing up and cooks for his father (who clearly treats Martyn as a sort of the domestic slave), we learn more about Alex and her mum. Alex's mum is an actress who was briefly famous for role in the television sitcom, but has fallen on hard times. Alex and Martyn have quite a lot in common: they both live in single parent families and in relative poverty; furthermore, it transpires that Alex's mum left Alex's dad because he had a drink problem. Now Alex's mum gets what work she can and the implication is clear – they struggle financially. In his thoughts about Alex, Martyn reveals something very significant: Alex has a clear idea of what she wants to be in life – an actress like her mother. Martyn's world seems so constricted and so narrow, an almost daily struggle for survival that he has never considered what career he might pursue. He tells us: 'what's impressed me most about Alex was her ambition. She had an ambition. She knew what she wanted to do, she wanted to be something' (p. 28). She is also a very good actress as she demonstrates to Martyn and does a completely convincing impersonation of Martyn's father on page 29.

Martyn has never even thought about what he might do in the future, but when pressed by Alex he says, somewhat prophetically as we will see, 'I want to be a writer. I'm going to write a murder mystery' (p. 29). Alex's brilliance impersonation of Martyn's father and her generally excellent acting skills work here as a kind of prolepsis in the light of later events.

The only source of conflict between Alex and Martyn appears to be Dean. On one occasion, when Martyn suggests to Alex that 'he is a bit of the dope isn't he?' (p. 30), we are told: 'Alex went mad. "How the hell would you know what he's like? You've only met him once! Christ!.... What's it got to do with you anyway? Who the hell do you think you are?"' (p. 30). However, one might question at this stage how far Alex is being sincere, or how much of her anger at Martyn is acting.

We now move into the sequence on page 30 which leads to Martyn's dad's death. Martyn is very familiar with the stages of his father's drunkenness, and thinks of them in four stages. The most dangerous stage is stage three in which Martyn's dad has a tendency to be violent: Martyn recalls an incident when he was much younger and his father hit his wrist so hard that his wrist was broken. Interestingly, despite his hatred of his father and despite his father's physical abuse of him, at the hospital and when being interviewed by the social worker, Martyn pretends that it was an accident in order to protect his father. Perhaps he is frightened of the alternatives: he has no contact with his mother, so the alternatives to living with his father are living with Aunty Jean (which he hates the idea of) or being taken into local authority care and put in an orphanage. Martyn is phlegmatic: he comments: 'the way I looked at it, things weren't perfect, but at least I knew where I was with dad. Better the devil you know than the devil you don't, as they say' (p. 33).

Martyn is trying to watch an episode of *Inspector Morse* on the television; in fact he reveals that the only things he watches on television are detective series or crime films. All the way through the program his father makes comments, intended to be amusing, which mock the events onscreen. Events reach a climax when his father repeats Morse's terse call to his assistant: "Lew-is! Lew-is! Lew-is!" (p. 35). Something in Martyn snaps and uncharacteristically he interrupts his father, saying: "Shut up!..... For God's sake, Dad, just shut up! It's not funny, it's pathetic. You're pathetic. Why can't you just shut your mouth and let me watch the bloody television for once?" (p. 35).

Martyn's anger makes his father respond by trying to punch him, but his father is so drunk that Martyn easily dodges the blow and as his father swings past, carried forward by his own momentum, Martyn shoves him in the back: 'That's all it was, a shove. Just a shove. An instinctive defensive gesture. No more. I didn't hit him or anything. All I did was push him away' (p. 36). Then Martyn's father flies across the room and falls, hitting his head on the fireplace wall – 'the sickening crack of bone on stone.... I knew he was dead. Instantly. I knew' (p. 36). Martyn intuitively senses that his father is dead: 'I knew he was dead. I could feel it. The air, the flatness, the lifelessness' (p. 37). For a minute he stands motionless with the television still on in the background. He is struck by what he calls 'the absence of drama in reality. When things happen in real life, extraordinary things, there's no music, there's no dah-dah-daaahhs...Nothing stops, the rest of the world goes on' (p. 37). This will not be the last time in the novel that Martyn contrasts real life with the heightened and artificial reality of television and film.

He then checks that his father really is dead by feeling on his neck and then listening for the sound of his heart. We feel that Martyn is being completely honest in his description of how his father dies; there are some study guides that suggests that Martyn is telling a version of events which puts him in a good light and which therefore makes him an unreliable narrator – someone telling the story whom we cannot fully trust. We address this question of Martyn's reliability, as the narrator, later in the discussion of his character: we feel for reasons that we explain later that he is reliable narrator and tells the truth concerning the events surrounding dad's death. What is more disturbing is Martyn's failure to administer the kiss of life (he has earlier told us that he's taken a first aid course at school so that he can tell when his father is simply comatose from drink from when he is genuinely dead) and his failure to call for an ambulance. He addresses these questions on page 38: 'Why didn't I ring 999, call out the emergency services?.... Why didn't you give him artificial respiration?.... Why didn't you try to save his life? (p. 38). Martyn answers his own questions by saying: 'I don't know. I just didn't. All right?' (p. 38), but we think as readers that now that his father is dead, albeit by a terrible accident, Martyn would prefer that he remains dead: after all, he hated him.

The circumstances of his father's death mean that in England Martyn would probably not be tried for murder, but rather manslaughter and, given that it was an accident and given his father's violent behaviour, there is every chance that Martyn would receive a suspended sentence. However, once his father is dead and he does not call for an ambulance, he is creating a massive problem for himself – why does he delay in informing the emergency services of his father's death? The delay in itself makes things look very suspicious, and the longer he delays, the harder it will be to explain his complete lack of action. We know that Martyn enjoys murder mysteries. We feel that he doesn't call for an ambulance because he is happy that his father is dead, but also that he prolongs the delay in a bizarre attempt to get into a difficult position from which he must use his wit and cunning to extricate himself.

Martyn knows what he should do and keeps staring at a telephone in guilt. The doorbell rings and Alex arrives. Martyn confesses to Alex what has happened and how it happened. When they look at Dad's body Alex takes charge, making Martyn cover him up with a sheet from the airing cupboard and putting her arms around him to comfort him:

That moment, when she held me... it was as if nothing else mattered. Nothing. Everything would be all right. Her soft hand on the back of my head, the comfort of her body close to mine... everything else just faded away into nowhere. This was where I wanted to be. (p. 41)

But in the next standalone, single sentence paragraph Martyn tells us – 'but nothing lasts for ever' (p. 41). Martyn, of course, means that Alex will have to stop holding him and return to her own house that night, but again, in retrospect as readers, we might see this as another moment of prolepsis. In the rest of the chapter Alex tries to persuade Martyn to make a telephone call to the police to let them know what has happened, but Martyn is adamant in his refusal. His delay in making the call makes him look more guilty, and, because he cannot explain, in any rational way, why he decided to delay the call, he is worried that he will end up in a home – '...they'll probably just put me in a loony bin' (p. 42). By now it is late at night and Brooks again uses pathetic fallacy to set the mood of this part of the story: it is raining heavily and the pure white snow has disappeared. Alex offers him a bed at her house for the night – a natural reaction because it is generally thought to be upsetting to be alone in a house with a dead body. However, Martyn shows his strength and resilience by refusing her offer and insisting that he will be all right. Alex goes home and once again in a moment of prolepsis 'she didn't look back' (p. 45)

This long opening chapter is very important as an introduction to the novel that follows. This chapter:

- introduces us to the central character and narrator and establishes what he is like;

- describes his unhappy home life with his boorish, slovenly, drunken father;

- introduces us to Alex and her unpleasant boyfriend, Dean;

- mentions Martyn's Aunty Jean – the only relative he has any contact with;

- sets up the rest of the plot - the accidental death of Dad – which Martyn fails to report to the authorities and the cover up of which will drive the rest of the plot.

Chapter Two: Thursday

The day starts with a disturbing dream, one in which Martyn's current fears are projected. He is being interviewed by the fictitious Inspector Morse for the shooting of his father; Alex betrays him and Morse is metamorphosed into his dying father, repeating his father's last words over and over again: 'Lewis! Lew-is!...'.

Martyn wakes from the dream screaming but then goes on to carry out the routine practices of a normal day – taking a bath, brushing his teeth and having breakfast. He takes time to contemplate his appearance: 'I was not a beauty. But then again, I wasn't exactly a hunchback, either.' (p. 48). His behaviour suggests that he is emotionally removed from his father's death. A little later his thoughts turn to the existential – the vagaries of human existence: 'fate, determinism, free will – that sort of thing.' (p. 49). He recounts the words of Einstein:

Everything is determined...the beginning as well as the end, by forces over which we have no control. It is determined for the insect as well as for the star. Human beings, vegetables or cosmic dust, we all dance to a mysterious tune, intoned in the distance by an invisible piper. (p. 49 – 50)

In essence, it appears that Martyn is trying to rationalise his father's death and absolve himself of any wrong-doing. (Note: The 'invisible piper' will recur in the text on four more occasions).

The post arrives and in amongst it there is a letter addressed to William Pig, Esq. which catches Martyn's attention: he opens it and learns that his father is the recipient of a cheque to the value of £30,000. His shock is evident in the repetition of the amount and the way the author has given each occurrence a fresh line which acts as a pause, emphasising Martyn's disbelief (p. 51):

£30,000.

A three and four zeros.

Thirty thousand pounds.

It is a bequest from a deceased Miss Eileen Pig. Martyn has no idea who this is, but he concludes that his father was not going to make him party to knowledge of the inheritance or, indeed, its benefits. Martyn decides to search inside the bureau in his father's unkempt bedroom, a place he has dim memories of from bygone Christmas mornings, before his mother left. He discovers that Miss Pig was his great aunt; he also discovers a valid cashcard on which the pin number has been written.

Having attended to his domestic chores Alex appears at the house. Again she implores Martyn to call the police, however, he rationalises that the time elapsed between his father's death and now would render him culpable. The author throws in a very subtle clue as to the novel's conclusion at this juncture, something which hints at Alex's true potential:

I turned to face Alex. For the briefest of moments I didn't recognise her, she was a stranger. But almost immediately the illusion lifted. It must have been the light or something. (p. 56)

Martyn goes on to tell Alex about the inheritance and the beginnings of a plan to dispose of the body are hatched – they will dump the body in a water-filled quarry: Alex will use her mother's car to get them there. There are two problems though: Alex cannot get hold of her mother's car until Saturday, and Aunty Jean is due to pay her annual visit tomorrow.

Alex leaves to meet up with Dean. Meanwhile as Martyn is 'moping' around, he realises that he has a new problem in that his father's corpse is beginning to smell: 'I wasn't quite sure whether this musty smell was just an ordinary dirty-drunk-peron-who-hasn't-washed-and-has-spent-the-night-lying-in-the-fire-place kind of smell, or if it was the start of something worse...an undertaker might be walking past.' (p. 62).

Alex returns with Dean who is now party to the fact that Martyn's father is both dead and the recipient of £30,000. He has bugged Alex's bag and has all the material he needs to perform an ugly machination on Martyn. Dean threatens to uncover the truth unless Martyn gets him the £30,000 by Monday. Martyn begins to put to work the information he has derived from his murder-mystery obsession in his own real-life murder-mystery, his mind is suddenly clear: 'I could see all the possibilities, I understood the probabilities, I'd calculated the odds...' (p. 71-72). Martyn tweezers Dean's fallen hair and abandoned cigarette from the linoleum floor and places them in an envelope. That night he sleeps soundly: 'There was nothing there to bother me. Nothing. I slept a long and dreamless sleep.'

This chapter:

- introduces the cheque of £30,000 – the catalyst to both Dean and Alex's cruel machinations;

- establishes the plot to dispose of Dad's body at the quarry using Alex's Mum's car;

- reveals Dean's plans to blackmail Martyn;

- concludes with Martyn's counter-blackmail – collecting Dean's discarded DNA in the form of hair and a cigarette butt to plant with his Dad's remains.

Chapter Three: Friday

The action of this chapter centres around the visit of Aunty Jean, and the tension created by the question of whether she will accept that her brother is alive. In its tone, however, while the chapter does contain tension, there are also moments of near farce and black humour, and passages of philosophical discussion between Martyn and Alex. There is another element as well: Alex is left alone for a long time in this chapter and it is only much later in the novel that the reader realises that she has used this time to make preparations to betray Martyn.

This chapter begins with Martyn and Alex having to move Dad's dead body from the living room upstairs into his bed. In life, Martyn comments, 'Dad wasn't that tall.... but dead he weighed a ton, and it took us the best part of an hour to get him up the stairs (p. 75). When a body is dead, rigor mortis sets in and this complicates their task: 'he was a bit stiff as well, and his arms and legs kept getting caught in the banisters, which didn't help. But we got him there in the end' (p.75). Martyn seems completely unaffected emotionally by moving his father's dead body and, as soon as they finish, he casually suggests to Alex that he should make a pot of tea. (p. 75).

As they drink their tea Martyn and Alex discuss the morality of what they have just done. Alex begins the discussion by asking 'Are we bad? (p. 75). Martyn counters by arguing that morality is relative: 'it's a relative kind of thing, badness.... Good, bad. Right, wrong. What's the difference? Who decides?' (p. 75). When Alex points out that what they've done is against the law, Martyn counters with 'What's the law? It's only someone's opinion' (p. 75). Alex tries to argue that there are certain acts such as murder and rape which are universally and unequivocally wrong, but Martyn will not even accept this and replies 'whatever anyone does, it's not wrong to them..... It's only wrong if you think it's wrong. If you think it's right, and others think it's wrong, then it's only wrong if you get caught' (p. 76). Given what Alex does to Martyn later in the novel and, more importantly, what she does to

Dean, Martyn's words here are shown to be both ironic and incorrect: some things are wrong; some things are immoral.

For most of the day Martyn waits for Aunty Jean, after discussing when Alex's mum's car will be available so that they can move dad's body from the house to the flooded quarry. Martyn enjoys the fact that Alex does not feel the need to talk incessantly; she is comfortable simply being with him and does not feel the need to break the silence with any mindless chatter. Martyn wonders what Alex is thinking about and concludes that you can never know what someone else is really thinking – that you cannot even be certain that other people perceive the same reality as you do. This paragraph on page 77 is another one which, in retrospect, can be seen ironically. We cannot be sure, but if we were to speculate about what Alex is really thinking about over tea in Martyn's kitchen, we might come to the conclusion (having reached the end of the novel) that she is thinking about all the things she needs to do in order to betray Martyn and get away with her theft of his money successfully.

They go back upstairs to prepare Dad's body for Aunty Jean's arrival and once again Alex behaves in rather strange ways (but the real significance of her behaviour cannot be seen until later). Alex applies make up to Dad's face so he looks alive, and Martyn's feelings for her rise in admiration: 'Look at that girl. Who else would do that for you? Who else? My heart sank' (p. 79). Martyn is aware of how ridiculous what they're doing is and remembers the imaginary games of his childhood when he pretended to be 'Martyn the Cowboy…. Martyn the Avenger, feared throughout the kingdom. Martyn the Assassin, cold eyed and calculating, a hunter. A killer' (p. 79). He mocks his younger daydreaming self and admits 'I don't remember doing anything. I just imagine things' (p. 79). This is more prolepsis: later in the novel the words 'Martyn the Assassin, cold eyed and calculating, a hunter. A killer' is going to be repeated at a key moment with only one word change on page 190. Martyn has already commented on page 78 on the sheer size of Alex's bag (which we later realize she must have put some of Dad's clothes in for her mother to use on her trip to the bank) and, on the same page, was she really putting Dad's clothes way in the wardrobe – or deciding which ones to steal, which ones her mother could later wear to the bank when they steal Martyn's money? Of course, at the time both Martyn and the reader are wholly unaware of these reasons for Alex's strange behaviour. Martyn attributes it to the trauma of handling a dead body and the tension they both feel over Aunty Jean's visit. There is even the possibility that that the reader might think that Alex is pregnant by Dean which would be another reason for her frequent need to use the bathroom to be sick in. In this context too, while Martyn is waiting for his aunt's arrival, Alex is wandering around upstairs on the pretext of feeling sick and needing to use the bathroom, but the noises she makes prompt Martyn to ask himself, 'What is she doing?' (p. 84). It is only much later that Martyn works out what she must have been doing: getting the things that she and her mother needed to steal the money successfully.

Aunty Jean's visit passes successfully and she believes that Dad is alive. Her questions to Martyn about his progress at school are presented as meddlesome and interfering, but it could be argued that she is showing genuine concern and interest in Martyn's welfare. She stays for a cup of tea and chats about her brother and their parents – full of criticism for Martyn's Dad. At the end of her visit she needs to use the toilet and this causes momentary tension because Alex is hiding in the bathroom. However, she has hidden behind the shower curtain and Aunty Jean's visit passes successfully: she leaves convinced that she has seen her brother alive – this is vital to the story that Martyn will tell to the police.

Once Alex has left, Martyn reflects on the poor quality of his life and the area he lives in, but snaps out of it when he thinks of what he and Alex can do with the £30,000. Two things are integral to his fantasy: being with Alex and leaving England. The fantasy culminates in Martyn imagining that they would end up on 'a small island. Right out in the middle of the sea where no one else could get to' (p. 96). This is further evidence of Martyn's distrust and disliking for other people.

Martyn has a fitful night's sleep and, as the readers are well aware, tomorrow he and Alex must dispose of Dad's body. All he can do is wait.

This chapter is generally positive and optimistic overall and in it:

- Aunty Jean's visit passes without mishap;

- the bonds between Martyn and Alex seem strengthened by their interplay and their shared tasks;

- Martyn and Alex discuss the morality of what they are doing once again;

- Martyn reveals his despair about his current life and his fantasies about the future with Alex and his £30,000;

- there are various examples of proleptic irony which pass unnoticed on a first read of the novel.

Chapter Four: Saturday

The chapter begins in the morning, four days before Christmas. Martyn gazes out of the window and observes his surroundings. He paints a picture of gloom and the frequent leitmotif of 'dead' peppers his description; 'Dead green... dead green spikes...a dead cigarette'. He observes a young family making their way to their car. The couple 'slouch', 'grunt' and the kids are 'snotty nosed' (p. 99). Martyn comments, sarcastically: 'Happy Christmas'.

The phone rings: it is Alex confirming that she can access the car later that day but she has to go shopping with her mother now.

Martyn decides that he needs some air, somewhere that 'isn't full of noise and ugliness' (p.100). Eliminating the town, he decides on the nearby beach. He collects the pound coins he had placed on his father's eyes to keep them shut and also some coins from his father's pockets for the bus fare.

Having reached the snow-covered beach Martyn's emotions oscillate wildly. On page 104 he feels happy and then on page 105 he pauses 'weighed down with a sudden sadness'. He continues to describe his surroundings with the bleak leitmotif of death: 'half-dead dog' (p. 104); 'The wind had died' (p. 104); 'a dead porpoise' (p. 105); 'If I sit here long enough, I thought, I'll die' (p. 107). This continues as Martyn experiences a moving vision. Alex appears on the beach: 'Gliding silently across the sea in a candle white dress...' (p. 108). Then the vision turns sinister and it is not Alex, 'It's Dad':

Staggering up the beach ridiculously dressed in size eight boots and a ragged white dress. Like a ghoulish scarecrow, deathly pale and drunk. Dad. With a can of shaving foam clutched in his out-stretched hand...lifeless but alive, dead eyes sunk into his wounded head. (p. 108)

Martyn runs through the snow until he reaches the road. He challenges us to believe his vision or dream as a reality: 'Believe it. Or don't. It's up to you. I don't really care. I know what happened' (p. 111). We can deduce from this, together with the oscillating emotions, that Martyn is a very disturbed boy.

He returns home wet and cold, and submerges himself into a hot bath. Alex arrives and Martyn greets her, a towel wrapped around him. He feels self-conscious and goes to get dressed. As Martyn is zipping up his trousers Alex presents him with surgical masks 'to keep the smell out.' Martyn contributes two pairs of rubber gloves – 'Fingerprints' he explains. The pair prepare the body, dressing Martyn's father and removing the makeup Alex had applied to convince Aunty Jean that he was not dead. Martyn lodges Dean's hair beneath his father's fingernails and empties the contents of the envelope into the sleeping bag – more of Dean's hair and the discarded cigarette butt. Having stapled the open end shut, they manoeuvre the body clumsily down the stairs.

Once the bag is sealed both Martyn and Alex refer to the bagged-up father as 'it': 'Give it a push' (p. 118) and 'It landed at the bottom of the stairs.' (p. 118). They have disassociated themselves from the real contents of the sleeping bag. They struggle to get the bag in the car, but eventually succeed. Martyn considers the possibility of being seen and refers back to the Invisible Piper:

If someone sees us, they see us. If they don't, they don't. That's all there is to it. It's that mysterious tune again, the invisible piper. He plays, we dance – what happens, happens. (p. 120)

Martyn and Alex then set off on a perilous journey to the pit: 'I didn't fancy driving through a snow storm in a wreck of a car, with a dead body in the back, driven by an underage wreck of a driver, with no licence and no insurance.' (p. 123)

Arriving at the pitch black pit, the author introduces another clue as the scene unfolds; Martyn observing Alex notes: 'I thought I saw a glimpse of something. Something blacker than anything else.' (p. 127-128). They break the icy surface of the water with rocks and insert more rocks into the sleeping bag to weigh it down. Finally, they push the laden bag over the edge of the precipice. Alex asks Martyn how he feels and he replies: 'Never felt better.' (p. 130)

As Alex drives them home Martyn ruminates on morality and reassures himself that he has done nothing wrong. He turns to the reader and says: 'Break it down, look at it, analyse my actions. What did I do? Did I kill? Did I steal? Did I covet my neighbour's ass?...' (p. 132)

He questions Alex's involvement with Dean. She responds circumspectly, clearly uneasy with the line of questioning. He abandons his inquiry and asks Alex whether Dean will get the money. Again, the author offers a clue or a foreshadowing to the unexpected conclusion or *denouement*:

'Oh no,' she said. 'He won't be getting the money.' And then she laughed, a curiously cold sound, almost vicious. If it had been anyone else but Alex, I think it might have scared me.

Remember, this is a reflective narrative, Martyn is recounting his own mystery story – trying to make sense of it and picking out the things he overlooked as the events unfolded. Oblivious at the time, arriving home he states: 'I felt a warm glow of comfort. Satisfied, happy, secure.' (p. 132) We know, in retrospect, that Martyn's feelings were entirely misguided.

The chapter concludes with Martyn's predisposition toward fatalism – (that is the belief that all events are predetermined and therefore inevitable or a submissive attitude to events as being inevitable):

I put my hands in my pockets and looked up at the stars. Everything is determined, the beginning as well as the end, by forces over which we have no control.

This chapter:

- deviates from the main plot with the extended beach scene – this allows the main character's oscillating emotions to be exposed;

- introduces the macabre vision of beautiful Alex morphing into Martyn's monstrous father – a portent to Alex's betrayal, perhaps;

- establishes Martyn's relationship with the concept of home: 'Home is home, I suppose. No matter how much you hate it. You still need it. You need whatever you're used to. You need security.' (p. 112);

- describes the preparation of Dad's body, the planting of Dean's DNA and then, finally, the disposal of the corpse in the quarry;

- provides clues as to Alex's seditious and covert intentions

(Dad's missing jacket and the description of her words and mannerisms on page 134: "'He won't be getting the money." And then she laughed, a curiously cold sound, almost vicious...'");

- expands upon the theme of fate and determinism.

Chapter Six: Sunday

This is a short reflective chapter and we gain a lot of insight into Martyn's state of mind. For him it is a wasted day as he waits all day for Alex to arrive and she does not. Towards the end of the chapter, while talking on the phone, Martyn realizes that she tells him a lie.

Martyn is woken by the discordant clanging of the bells from the local church, which once again shows his desire for quietness and peace. There is a humorous touch when he remarks 'Don't they know it's Sunday? People are trying to sleep' (p. 136). As readers we imagine that Martyn, despite criticizing the sound of the bells, is well aware that they are ringing only because Sunday is the Christian Sabbath, although in secular Britain most people see Sunday as a good excuse for a lie-in. Martyn's critical, almost misanthropic attitude is even shown when he tells us that he once saw the bell-ringers – 'a bunch of sad looking vegetarian types with beards and long arms. Bell-ringer's arms. Perhaps that's where they drink – the Bellringers Arms. Ho Ho.' (p. 136). Martyn's awareness that he has made an awful joke endears him to the reader.

Martyn has left almost all the windows open and relishes the fact that the house smells only of 'cold clean December air – no cigarette smoke, no stale beer, no whisky, no sweaty clothes, no *Vaporub*, no dead bodies.... Beautiful' (p. 137). When he gets up and looks out of the window he realizes that it has snowed again overnight. The unpleasant, rundown, poor part of town that Martyn lives in has been transformed by the purity of the snow: 'I smiled. Everything was clean and white – cars, walls, the road, the pavements. All the muck and dirt was hidden beneath sheer white blankets of snow' (p. 137).

However, Martyn acknowledges sadly that it wouldn't last long. 'By this afternoon it'd just be wet, grey, mushy mess. Why can't they just leave it alone' (p. 137). Once again Martyn shows his preference for the natural world over the built environment created by human beings: he also expresses his sadness and incredulity at people's obsession with clearing up the fallen leaves of autumn: 'Why does everybody rush around dementedly sweeping up every little leaf that falls to the ground? Sweep 'em up, brush 'em up, pile 'em up and burn 'em. Burn the buggers! Burn them all before it's too late! They're all mad (p. 137).

Martyn meticulously makes himself breakfast while listening to Desert Island Discs on the radio (which is quite an unusual choice for a teenage boy we might note). After careful consideration, Martyn comes to the conclusion that he would take no favourite records, no favourite novel and no luxury item to his desert island: 'there was nothing I wanted on my desert island, nothing at all' (p.138) We think this shows Martyn's sense of self-reliance and independence: his impoverished lifestyle and his need to do so many things for himself, have combined to make him resourceful and self-contained.

After breakfast he goes into the front room of the house and, as if for the first time, he says he notices how poor and worn and faded everything is. 'The wallpaper, the furniture, carpets, the armchairs, the joke television, like something out as the 1950s' (p. 139). This description has the effect of reinforcing, yet again, the extreme poverty that Martyn lives in, but the fact that he only notices these things now seems to suggest that he has been liberated in some way by his father's death. His mind is still dwelling on the murder though: Brooks makes it clear that Martyn is still dwelling on details from the evening of his father's death. For example, when Martyn looks at the phone, Brooks inserts the following sentence in italics – '*Go on, before it's too late*' (p. 140) – which is something Martyn said to himself following his father's death; when Martyn looks at the fireplace he comments 'I remembered the sound, bone on stone, that hollow crack. Bloodstone. Cold and hard and clean and deadly (p. 140).

Eventually Martyn's frustration leads him to call Alex's house only to be told by her mother that she is out visiting a friend. In the meantime Martyn has some thinking to do (p. 141) and mentions his plan to deal with Dean: this creates interest and tension in the reader because we do not know, and Martyn does not reveal, what his plan is. After two more hours, his anxiety clearly increasing, he calls Alex's house again, but this time no one answers.

Throughout the chapter Brooks has kept reminding us of the passage of time by the use of single sentence paragraphs stating exactly what the time is. We reach five o'clock and it is dark. In stark contrast to the many rather ugly and dispiriting descriptions of human beings and the world Martyn lives in, he describes the setting of the sun in a beautiful, almost poetic way, once again showing his enthusiasm for the natural world:

Sunset. The blood red disc of the sun outlined against a flat sky, the sky a dull glow of pearl-grey light. The sinking sun throwing out threads of colour as it dies, reaching up into the dark, like a drowning man throwing up his arms, reaching out for something that isn't there. Then down it goes, vast and perfect, burning down into the sunrise of another time, another world. And when it's gone, the patient black water of the night steals in and up crawls the moon. (pp. 141 – 142)

We have quoted this at length because it is such a beautiful and convincing description: Martyn loves nature, but he is cynical and misanthropic towards humanity and most of the human world.

At six he rings Alex again and even crosses the street to hear his phone ringing in her house, but it is obvious that there is no one home. Feeling bored he turns on the television set, but typically is annoyed and distracted by the '...shouting, stupid music, adverts' (p. 142). And then in a brief digression about his father, he makes it clear that as far as he's concerned Dad simply does not exist anymore which suggests that Martyn has no belief in an afterlife.

Nine o'clock arrives and Martyn watches the clock slowly tick round to 9:05. At 9.30 a car pulls up outside which raises his hopes, but it turns out to be two young men who are going to visit Don the drug dealer who lives in Martyn's road.

Martyn reveals that when he was a child, he tried to imagine what it would be like to be dead and, confirming that he has no belief in an afterlife, he admits that what really frightened him was the total absence of everything. 'No life, no darkness or light, nothing to see, nothing to feel, nothing to know, no time, no where or when, no nothing, forever. It was so unimaginable it was frightening' (p. 144). This thought would make him burst into tears and he admits that, although he no longer cries, nothing much has changed – 'I'm still that little kid lying in bed at night looking for the emptiness' (p. 144). Why does Brooks choose to tell us about Martyn's childhood fears at this point? Surely it's to demonstrate his vulnerability and his anxiety over the fact that he has not spoken to Alex all day, despite their arrangement to do so. He is alone and he doesn't know where his closest friend is, and so these melancholic thoughts come back to him to show the despair that he is feeling at this moment.

He then tells us that the year before he had thrown out all his belongings – 'toys, games, boxes full of comics, clothes, pictures, posters' – and now the room is just how he likes it (p. 145). Martyn's predilection for neatness and order could not be shown more clearly in the neat and spartan arrangement of his room.

Finally the phone rings and, after waiting all day, Martyn eventually gets to speak to Alex, but what she says adds a distinct note of tension to the end of the chapter. She lies to Martyn: she says that she did not come round in the morning because she and her mother were visiting one of her mother's friends – Martyn knows this to be a lie because he spoke to Alex's mother that very morning. There have been other hints of things going wrong, but these have been examples of proleptic irony used by Brooks which only become ironic when we have read the whole novel and look back; they could be said to foreshadow, in a very general way, later events. Alex's lie to Martyn is different, because both Martyn and the reader know that it is a lie.

Martyn decides to give up on Sunday but cannot sleep; he does not discuss the lie but he has noticed it (he remarks to the reader, 'She wasn't out with her mum this morning' p. 146) and perhaps this is because of his sleeplessness. He takes Raymond Chandler's *The Big Sleep* and 'reads and reads and reads' until finally he falls asleep with 'my head resting on the open novel' (p. 147).

This short, reflective chapter:

- gives further insight into Martyn's liking for order and cleanliness;

- shows how dependent he is on Alex – he waits all day for contact from her;

- increases tension as we, like Martyn, wonder and worry why Alex has not been in touch;

- introduces an element of doubt and worry when Alex lies about her whereabouts on Sunday morning.

Chapter Five: Monday

The chapter begins in the morning with Martyn's rambling musings on what happens while you sleep. He hears a milk float and someone calling out a dog's name. He then hears the milkman whistling and tries to whistle himself. While he eats his breakfast he looks out of the window, something which he often does. He recounts the time he killed a bird, which left him feeling '...cold. Ashamed. Scared. Dirty and bad.' (p. 150) There is no reference made to the events which have unfolded, perhaps this is avoidance on Martyn's part.

Alex arrives and Martyn observes that she seems distracted and hesitant. She apologises for not coming around the day before putting it down to the situation: 'I just needed to get away from it all for a while...this whole situation...it's pretty crazy. We disposed of a *body* for Christ's sake...' (p. 151) Again, in retrospect we can put her mannerisms down to something entirely different, namely her deceit and the secret machinations she has devised with her mother.

While they eat breakfast together they discuss accessing the money. Martyn demonstrates how well he can forge his father's signature and suggests that they use cheques to buy things until the money is cleared for withdrawal. Alex insists that they stick to the original plan: '...cheques are traceable. Cheques are dangerous.' (p. 153) It is clear that Alex has thought about this. Martyn agrees with Alex who then says she needs to use the bathroom. She takes the cash card, telling Martyn she will put it back into the bureau. She also takes the piece of paper with the forged signatures saying: 'You don't want to leave this lying around, do you? I'll flush it.' (p. 153). Of course, we now know that Alex visiting the bathroom was a ruse to take the cash card and signatures.

Martyn thanks Alex. She responds with laughter which Martyn finds perturbing:

It bothered me sometimes, the way she changed. One second this; the next second that. It was hard to keep up. But then we all have our odd little ways, I suppose. (p. 154)

Again, we know that Martyn's response, his gratitude, is entirely misplaced - having completed the novel. This is another instance of proleptic irony – something which at first glance has no element of irony; but which becomes ironic retrospectively when we learn of

Alex's secret agenda. At the time Martyn is simply aware that Alex's mannerisms can be surprising: he is not aware of her duplicity or the fact that she represents the antagonist.

Martyn walks Alex to the bus stop. Dean is due in an hour to claim the money. Martyn checks that Alex has the key to Dean's flat. As Alex boards the bus Martyn watches her, and we notice the repetition of the word 'watch' on page 155. This serves to add emphasis to Martyn's love and admiration for Alex:

I watched her pay...I watched the bus ticket snicker out. I watched the way her eyes blinked slowly...I watched the coal black shine of her hair. And I watched and waited in vain for her to turn her head as the bus lurched out into the street.

But, in another case of proleptic irony: 'She didn't look back.'

Martyn returns home and begins his ritualistic cleaning. Dean arrives and Martyn appears to take pleasure in antagonising him - his contempt is clear describing Dean as 'Six feet of wet dough' (p. 159) Martyn engages Dean in a conversation about Alex before telling him that he will not be the recipient of the money. He explains how he and Alex have framed Dean with forensics and tells Dean that Alex is at his flat searching for copies of the tape recording. Martyn goes to the window and notices that there is a trail of footprints leading towards Dean's bike. This is another clue Martyn overlooks at the time and we can assume retrospectively that this is when Alex tampered with Dean's brakes.

As Dean leaves in defeat, Martyn's last words to him could almost constitute a portent: '"I thought you'd gone", I said.' (p. 164)

Martyn listens to the noise of Dean's bike as he drives away from the house: 'One second, a faint waspish whining; the next second nothing. Gone. Odd, I thought.' He puts this down to 'some kind of acoustic illusion', but we know that the noise stopping abruptly is when Dean has his fatal crash. When Alex returns her behaviour is unusual 'like a sleepwalker'. She rubs her hands together repeatedly and appears unable to hear Martyn. Martyn notices a black smear on her hand, another clue which he overlooks at the time. During this time the noise of an ambulance is heard by both of them and Alex mutters something under her breath.

Eventually Alex seems to snap out of her trance and kisses Martyn: '...kissed me with ice cold lips.' (p. 166) She then goes to the bathroom and turns on the taps. Martyn puts this down to her being sick again and attributes this in turn to the shock. As a reader we might assume that Alex's frequent visits to the bathroom and her sickness indicate she is pregnant, it is only in retrospect that we realise that these are the occasions when she has been either manipulating evidence or gathering the documents necessary to access the money for herself. It is at this stage, we can assume, that she transferred the brake fluid to the facecloth. When she returns downstairs, she is back to her old self again: 'Smiling, bright and breezy, fresh. Clean' (p. 166).

Alex and Martyn discuss Dean's visit and Alex confirms that she has the tapes. Martyn admits that he is proud of himself and takes ownership of the events: 'Me. My plan. My idea' (p. 167). But when he asks Alex about whether they will see Dean again, he again observes something enigmatic about her:

She looked away, but not before I saw that funny look cross her face once more. It was like a face beneath a mask, revealed in an instant, then gone again. Too quick to recognise. (p. 167)

Alex and Martyn then begin a game of Scrabble, while Martyn ponders about how they will spend the money. Alex spends a long time making her moves, but Martyn is just happy to look at her. He observes that: 'She always concentrates right up to the end, taking ages over each word, thinking things through, not making her move until she's absolutely sure...' (p. 171) The irony in Martyn's observation is that Alex has adopted the same methodology in her plot to kill Dean and take Martyn's money. Martyn plucks up the courage to ask Alex whether she would like to go travelling with him. Her response is non-committal and she suggests that they discuss it tomorrow.

As she leaves she kisses Martyn again, this time on the cheek: 'The touch of her kiss on my cheek grew colder with every step she took.' (p. 173) This could be seen as symbolic of Alex's betrayal. Martyn questions whether he ever really knew her and, once again, refers to her not looking back:

I stood in the doorway for a while, waiting, but she didn't look back.
She never looked back.

This is a repetition of the proleptic irony on page 155:

And I watched and waited in vain for her to turn her head as the bus lurched out into the street. She didn't look back.

The chapter concludes as Martyn confirms this is the last time he saw Alex.

This chapter:

- reveals Martyn's feelings about taking the life of a bird, which left him '...cold. Ashamed. Scared. Dirty and bad.' (p. 150). Furthermore, it reveals that despite the fact that he had disposed of the bird's body, being out of sight did not allow him to forget about it. Although there is not direct reference to his Dad here, we know that the bird is representative of him;

- Alex arrives at the house and unbeknown to Martyn takes both the cash card and Martyn's forged signatures;

- after Alex's departure (ostensibly on a mission to retrieve the tapes), Dean arrives expecting to extract the money from Martyn, he is defeated, having learnt that Martyn has planted his DNA in the sleeping bag;

- Martyn observes a trail of footprints leading to Dean's bike. As the bike draws away the noise of the engine suddenly ceases which Martyn puts down to an 'acoustic illusion';

- a distracted Alex returns with fingers smeared black. In the distance the sound of sirens can be heard;

- having composed herself, the two of them play Scrabble and Martyn suggests that they use the money to 'go somewhere'. Alex response is guarded and she suggests that they talk about it tomorrow;

- most significantly, this chapter introduces all the clues necessary to implicate Alex in her betrayal of Martyn and in the killing of Dean;

- we learn that Alex 'never looked back' and that this '...was the last time I ever saw her.' (p. 173).

Chapter Seven: Tuesday

This is a crucial chapter in the development of the plot and it is vital because in it, Martyn comes to a realization of what has really happened and what Alex and her mother have done.

Martyn starts the day by being annoyed that Alex does not come round to his house first thing in the morning. But this stage he is not worried:

'Alex was often late' (p. 174). He also reveals his deep feelings for Alex by admitting that he is tolerant of her lateness: 'if you like someone enough, it doesn't matter how long they keep you waiting – as long as later in the end it's all right' (p. 174). Martyn's concern for punctuality is in keeping with his propensity for cleanliness and order, which in themselves might be said to be a reaction to the disorder and chaos and untidiness of his life with his father. As he says: '*I'm* never late for anything. I always make sure I'm early, then if something does happen, I've still got time to get wherever I'm going. If I can do it, why can't everyone else?' (p. 174). However, the reader knows from the end of the previous chapter that she will not turn up, that Martyn has already seen her for the last time, so we watch Martyn's tortured waiting with a sense of deep irony - dramatic irony, since we know more than the character reveals at this point in the novel. He is trying to describe his feelings and growing anxiety on that particular day, but we know that Monday night was the last time he ever saw her. This is bound to create even more sympathy and empathy for Martyn.

At this stage of the narrative Martyn is still fantasising about escaping from his humdrum and poor lifestyle by running away with Alex: 'I wanted out of here. Now. Just go, get on a train, a boat, a plane, get on and go. Anywhere. I told her that' (p. 174). As the morning goes on Martyn becomes increasingly frustrated: 'it was nine thirty. Where the hell was she? I waited. Ten minutes, twenty minutes, half an hour. I rang her. No answer' (p. 174).

At 10:30 he walks across to her house and realises that the house is completely empty and that there are no tyre tracks or footsteps in the snow, suggesting that no one has been at the house for quite some time. On the doorstep are two full milk bottles: no one is there to take them in.

It is at this moment that Martyn allows a shred of doubt to enter his mind: 'maybe I was waiting in vain. Maybe... No. She wouldn't do that.

Don't even think about it' (p. 176). At this point Brooks builds tension in the reader's mind because we do not know exactly what is going through Martyn's head.

Martyn consoles himself with the thought that Alex and her mother are using the car and that perhaps they are stranded somewhere in the snow without access to a telephone or that the car has broken down or that they could be in an accident. And he keeps telling himself, as if to reassure himself: '...don't even think about it. Don't even think about it' (p. 176).

The next two pages (176 & 177) are a masterpiece of writing on Kevin Brooks's part. Martyn very slowly comes to the realisation of what has happened and what Alex has done to him. Brooks' writing is so adept for two main reasons: firstly, almost all of these two pages are made up of single sentence paragraphs which reflect the slow realisation that Martyn comes to and the short single paragraphs help reflect his thoughts as he slowly comes to his dreadful conclusion; secondly, mixed in with Martyn's thoughts at that moment, are quotations from earlier in the novel printed in italics which have a generally ironic effect. They are ironic in two senses: firstly, some of them show the misplaced loyalty and trust which Martyn has demonstrated in Alex earlier in the novel – and which, in the light of Martyn's realisation, become darkly ironic, because they are so misplaced, and, secondly, many of the quotations from earlier in the text are now revealed to be examples of proleptic irony – in other words, we only realise that they are ironic in the light of later events; another way of looking at proleptic irony is to see it as a way the author uses to hint at future events or to foreshadow a truth that is yet to be revealed. Martyn's slow and agonising deduction (a method of deduction which he owes to all the crime novels that he has read) comes as a genuine shock to Martyn and to the reader. Brooks, by using Martyn as a first person narrator who does not know completely what is going on, is able to bring about the shocking revelations of this chapter.

Examples of earlier quotations that Brooks uses on these pages and which show Martyn's misplaced loyalty and affection for Alex are, for example: 'look at her, look at that girl. Who else would do that for you?' (p. 177), and all the apparently unselfish help that she gave Martyn to help convince Aunty Jean that his father was dead. There are more examples of proleptic irony: 'Tell me what you want me to be and I'll be it…. She can do anything: voices, the way people walk, posture, anything. She's brilliant' (p. 177) – the last two sentences being a comment about Alex's mum. Martyn also remembers things which Alex said which at the time seemed natural and helpful, but now, with his new-found realisation, can be seen as part of a plan to betray Martyn and defraud him of his money. The point is not simply that Martyn makes this terrible realisation for himself – that he works it out and has to deal with the knowledge that someone he felt great affection and trust for has betrayed him completely; the point is that Brooks's writing in these pages makes us feel Martyn's confusion and his slow realisation more vividly.

These memories from the past are mixed in with Martyn going to his father's bedroom and realising that his father's cheque book and cash card are missing as are his birth certificate, his marriage certificate, his medical card and all the solicitors' letters confirming the bequest. Some of his clothes are missing too. He is still confused and in a state of disbelief on page 179 and quotes Sherlock Holmes: 'When you have eliminated the impossible, whatever remains, however improbable, must be the truth'. At one stage he even tries to convince himself that Alex and her mother have taken the money in order to present it to him as a surprise or that Alex's mum, impersonating Martyn's father, has been arrested – but if that happens, Martyn reasons, the police would have been in his house a long time ago. On page 180 Martyn finally faces the truth:

Whatever remains is the truth. They've gone. She's gone. Taken the money and gone. Ripped you off. Conned you. Used you. Betrayed you. It was all an act. She's an actress. How could you ever have thought anything else? You, Martyn pig, with Alex? Beautiful Alex. No chance. Not in a million years. What have you got to offer?

Momentarily he thinks that Dean must have been involved in the conspiracy, but realises that can't be the case because Alex has helped frame Dean for his father's murder. Nonetheless, Martyn's pained and distraught sense of confusion and betrayal is captured well on page 181 with the single sentence, sometimes single word paragraphs, which vividly portray his sense of betrayal:

Where is she? What's she doing? What am I going to do? What can I do? Did I ever mean anything to her? Alex? Answer me. Tell me what happened. Tell me what you've done. Tell me it's impossible. Tell me. Please. (p. 181)

At midnight the doorbell rings and such is Martyn's emotional turmoil that all these anxieties are swept away and he seems to think his caller must be Alex, but is it is two policeman who want to question him about his father's murder and his friendship or otherwise with Dean West. Martyn is in trouble and does his best to evade the policeman's questions by lying or by telling half-truths. However, Detective Inspector Breece does reveal that Dean West has died in a motorcycle accident which the police are treating as murder because the brake lines on Dean's motorbike had been cut. Martyn claims that he barely knew Dean, but Breece's subordinate Detective Sergeant Finlay finds oil on a flannel in Martyn's bathroom – a fact which appears to contradict what Martyn has said. This, together with the fact that Martyn is under 16 and cannot be allowed to stay in the house alone, mean that the police have no option but to take him to the police station for the night.

They arrive at the police station at one o'clock in the morning on Christmas Day, and, paradoxically, given the situation that Martyn finds himself in, he notices the neatness and order of the police station's exterior:

The police station was clean and brightly lit. A low, pale brick building at the edge of town, it was surrounded by sparse lawns and smooth sloping driveway is. A calming place. It was quiet. An oasis in the desert of small-town noise. (pp. 187 – 188)

Because no one is available from social services to attend the police interview with Martyn, because he is under 16, the interrogation has to wait for the morning. He is too young to be detained in a cell, so they put him in a room with a proper bed, a carpet and even a television. As soon as he is on his own Martyn reveals to the reader what he is sure has happened. He even comments: 'I should have known. I would have known. If it was a story, a murder mystery, I would have spotted the clues, I would've worked out what was happening. It was obvious. (p. 189). He realises that Alex has cut the brake lines on Dean's motorbike – which explains the footprints which leads to Dean's bike in the snow and also the black smear on Alex's fingers – oil from Dean's motorbike. He even guesses that while she was upstairs in the bathroom washing off the oil, she also took the opportunity to steal the cheque book, the cheque card and the clothes from his father's room which she puts in the spacious bag that she always carries with her.

With genuine shock, Martyn realises that Alex was 'an assassin. Alex the Assassin, cold eyed and calculating, a Hunter, a killer...' (p. 190). Martyn attempts to rationalise it, by explaining or by trying to explain Alex's feelings towards Dean:

Alex had killed Dean. Killed him. It wasn't an accident. It wasn't unintentional. It wasn't just one of those things. It was a premeditated act of revenge. He'd humiliated her, he'd made her feel like nothing. He'd used her. And he had to pay. I could understand that. I'd felt the same way myself. But killing him? No. It was too much. (p. 191)

Even here Martyn is slightly mistaken, because Dean's murder is not an act of revenge for the way he has treated Alex; it is a way to remove any blame for Dad's death from Martyn, but, more importantly, to facilitate Alex's escape with the money. At this moment in the novel on page 191 Martyn reveals that there is a sense of morality inside him: the thought of Alex's premeditated murder of Dean makes him vomit copiously in the toilets and he tells us that 'something gripped me that night, and whatever it was it turned me inside out' (p. 191). He is plagued that night by the imagined details of Dean's crash into the side of the bus and by Alex rubbing her hands together again and again on her return to his house, having watched Dean's death: is this rubbing of the hands a sign of satisfaction at a task successfully concluded? Is it meant to remind us of that famous fictional assassin who could not stop rubbing her hands – Lady Macbeth?

Martyn speculates rather idly on how and when the idea of stealing the money came to Alex and her mother. More importantly, he starts to worry about the papers that Alex planted at Dean's flat – the solicitor's letters and the forged signatures. As the chapter closes the great unresolved mystery is whether Alex is trying to implicate Dean or Martyn in Martyn's father's death. Martyn is potentially in a very vulnerable position.

In many ways, although not the end of the story, this chapter:

- Allows Martyn to understand what Alex has done;
- Leaves Martyn in a precarious position awaiting questioning by the police on the following day;
- Is very exciting in the way is shows Martyn's thought processes as he finally sees the truth;
- Leaves us on a knife-edge: has Alex framed Martyn or Dean for the death of Martyn's father?

Chapter Eight: Christmas Day

Christmas Day

Martyn begins his Christmas Day in the police station. He has not slept, having been preoccupied with thinking things through. Breece arrives looking dishevelled. With him is the 'kind-faced' WPC Sally Sanders. Breece announces that Martyn's missing father has been found dead. Martyn had not anticipated his father being found so soon and struggles to decide how to respond in the absence of any true mourning – he tells himself that he knows nothing about it and pretends to cry. He is aware of Breece's scepticism: 'Breece was studying me, I could tell. The sympathetic look on his face couldn't hide the doubt in his eyes...' (p. 195).

After Breece has disclosed details concerning the location of the body, he announces the arrival of Martyn's aunt. Martyn refuses to see his aunt and eventually the two police officers leave him alone, as he has requested.

Alone again, Martyn congratulates himself on his performance: 'Not bad, not bad at all. Pretty convincing.' (p. 197). He then recounts the story behind his crocodile tears. Alex had taught him how to conjure up a really sad memory as a catalyst for tears. He then tells the pitiful tale of when his father sold his beloved dog Jacko 'down the pub'. This turns Martyn's attention back again to his father: 'He was a bastard, my dad, he really was.' (p. 197).

After Sally arrives with a cup of tea, Martyn begins to consider the many problems he now faces: The fact that Dean, the framed party, is now dead; potential evidence in the house; the fact that Martyn had lied about Dean. He likens the situation to a raggedy old pile of knots. He admits it's not a tidy situation like it is in his murder-mysteries.

Next Martyn finds himself in the interview room, it's not as he imagined it: 'No hooked nosed Sherlock Holmes staring down at me with cruel eyes. It was just a room, an ordinary looking office room...' (p. 200).The interview commences with a Peter Bennett from Social Services in attendance, together with another police officer, Detective Sergeant Donald Finlay. Martyn's responses are evasive until the subject of Dean is raised. Martyn then constructs a factitious story set at a Christmas end-of-term dance. He had been talking to a girl who, it transpired, was Dean's girlfriend. Martyn tells the officers that Dean threatened him and later came around to his house with another biker to repeat the threats. As Martyn's story gains momentum, it sees Dean rummaging around the house looking for cash and eventually emerging from Martyn's father's room carrying letters with 'a mad grin on his face'. Martyn tells the officers that the letters concerned his father's inheritance and that Dean had demanded the money by the following Monday. Martyn also claims that before this he knew nothing of the inheritance.

Monday arrives and Dean, true to his word, also arrives. Martyn recounts how he tried to explain to Dean that he hadn't been able to get hold of the money. Dean is 'furious, ranting and raving' and telling Martyn that he is 'dead meat' (p. 207). Martyn's fanciful tale continues with Dean visiting the bathroom and then his father's bedroom again: he emerges carrying a rucksack. Martyn adds with fabricated innocence: 'I think he was nicking stuff'. (p. 207).When Breece questions Martyn as to whether he went anywhere near Dean's motorbike, Martyn refers again to the phantom biker who may or may not have accompanied Dean: '...Unless there was someone on the back of it when he arrived, you know, the one who was with him on Thursday' (p. 207).

The interview finally concludes and Martyn, after some resistance, allows Bennett to take him to his aunt's house. His final thoughts turn to Alex: 'You thought of everything, didn't you?' (p. 211).

In this chapter:

- Martyn is officially informed of his father's demise;

- Martyn considers the complexities of his situation;

- in the interview Martyn fabricates a story around Dean, implicating him as solely responsible for his father's death and suggesting that he himself is entirely innocent of any wrong-doing;

- at the end of the interview the police tell him how his father's body was discovered: "Anonymous phone call'… 'Three o'clock this morning from a stolen mobile phone. Gave us the precise location of the body. Male voice…" (p. 210);

- Martyn is finally made totally clear as to Alex's involvement and the chapter concludes with: 'Alex. You thought of everything, didn't you?' (p. 211).

Chapter Nine: Epilogue

The final chapter entitled 'Epilogue' is set several months after the rest of the narrative and acts as a way of tying together some of the loose strands of the novel. In this sense it is very similar to modern detective fiction where the final chapter is often set a few months after the end of the main narrative and brings us up to date with what has happened to the characters. It is also similar to a modern detective novel in the sense that it contains a final twist which confirms many of Martyn's suspicions about Alex's role in the events that form the main narrative.

Martyn is living with his Aunty Jean and, in keeping with his stoical attitude, he admits 'it's not as bad as I thought it would be' (p. 212); although he goes on to say 'although that's not to say it's great or anything. There's plenty of Aunty's crap to deal with' (p. 212). In one sense Aunty Jean is trying to widen Martyn's interests, because all he wants to do is lie in bed and read detective novels. He is also annoyed by her need to know where he's going and who he's been with; but as

Martyn writes 'not that it really matters, I hardly ever go anywhere. And when I do I don't tell her anything. I just lie. But still, it gets on my nerves' (p. 212).

He grudgingly admits that 'At least her house is quite nice' (p.212), and, although he does not expand on this remark, it is clear that it is a complete contrast to the home he shared with his father.

There is a very ironic revelation, because it turns out that Aunty Jean is a drunkard just as her brother was. She pretends that she is merely a social drinker, but Martyn is aware that she has bottles of alcohol hidden all over the house. However, unlike Billy's father, she is not a violent drunk – the alcohol makes her tearful and maudlin. Martyn comments in his stoical, accepting way: 'it's all right, I don't really mind' (p. 213).

Martyn reveals more hypocrisy when he recounts his father's funeral – 'which I hated' (p. 213). He comments 'it was terrible. Sitting in this stupid chapel with a load of people I didn't know (p. 213). Most of the congregation were 'strangers. Strangers in a strange place' (p. 213). In the finest tradition of modern detective novels Detective Inspector Breece attends the funeral: this always seems to happen in detective novels, as though by observing the congregation at the funeral the detective hopes to notice some unusual or out of place behaviour which might give him a clue as to the identity of the murderer. Martyn dislikes the service even more: the music, the hymns, the prayers, and in particular the vicar talking about what a good man William Pig was when he was alive – which the reader knows is complete nonsense.

According to Martyn, the case is still officially open (p. 214). Breece's instincts tells him that he hasn't really solved the case. Martyn comments 'he knew I had *something* to do with it, but he couldn't work out what. I think he was pretty sure that Dean killed dad.... As to who killed Dean, I think he had me pegged for that' (p. 214). However,

Breece can prove nothing, despite his instincts, his gut feeling that Martyn was deeply involved in what had happened. In addition, Martyn remarks – 'as to what happened to the £30,000 I don't think Breece had a clue' (p. 215). There is some video footage of a figure resembling Martyn's father cashing a cheque for £30,000 on the Tuesday morning. But who could it be? Martyn's father and Dean were both dead by Tuesday morning and it could not have been Martyn because he is too short to pass himself off as his father. Martyn gives us an interesting insight into the workings of justice:

You see, it doesn't matter what the police think, it doesn't matter what they know, all that matters is proof. If they can't prove something, there's nothing they can do. Nothing. They're stuffed. That's the way it is, that's the way it works. That's justice. (p. 216)

After about three months, interest in the case fades since the police are making no progress, but Martyn has one more interesting interview with Detective Inspector Breece in April. The setting is beautiful and this is a reminder to the reader that Martyn's life has changed completely since he lived in the dilapidated, dirty and messy house that he shared with his father. 'Spring sunshine flooded in through the open conservatory doors, a smell of fresh flowers breezed in the air' (p. 216). For the first time in the investigation Breece mentions Alex, or Alexandra Freeman. The police have been looking at the phone records and have noticed that Martyn and Alex phoned each other a great deal during the Christmas period. Martyn fobs Breece off with an excuse about Alex helping him during the holidays on a school project. There are a few minutes of silence but outside; 'it was a beautiful day. Cloudless blue skies, willow trees waving gently in a slow breeze, birds singing' (p. 218). Brooks is using pathetic fallacy here to reflect Martyn's new-found stability at Aunty Jean's house, but also to suggest that Martyn has lied successfully to the police and that, no matter what Breece thinks, there is absolutely nothing he can do. Breece leans forward in his chair and says softly to Martyn 'How does it feel,

Martyn?....getting away with murder' (p. 218). Martyn remains calm and simply replies 'I don't know what you mean' (p. 218).

The final two pages of the novel bring the narrative to a close. Martyn receives a letter through the post from Alex which reveals that she and her mother have used the £30,000 to start a new life in the USA and that Alex has her first role as a paid actress – in an advertisement for a deodorant. However, she has also got auditions for proper parts too – in films and in the theatre.

In a strange way, Alex's letter breaks the habits that she has developed throughout the novel of not looking back. By writing to Martyn she is, in a figurative sense, looking back at the past and trying to justify her actions. Early in the letter she writes 'I tried to leave things pointing in the right direction' (pp. 219 – 220) – a reference to framing Dean for Dad's murder and ensuring that Dean's murder could not be connected with Martyn. Interestingly, she also refers to something that Martyn once said and which raises the whole question of morality:

You told me once that badness is a relative thing – you said that something's only wrong if you think it's wrong. That if you think it's right, and others think it's wrong, then it's only wrong if you get caught. I didn't understand what you meant at the time. But now, I think I do. I hope you still believe it. If not... Well, what can I say? (p. 220).

For us as readers this clarifies the novel's debate into morality and calls into question what Martyn originally said. Alex has stolen £30,000 from someone who regarded her as his only friend: surely this is wrong? Not only that: she has murdered someone in order to achieve her aims.

Martyn reacts calmly and placidly to Alex's letter. The last two sentences – written as two separate paragraphs – read:

I put down the letter and looked out of the window.

It was starting to snow. (p. 220)

Some readers have speculated why Martyn shows so little anger or resentment on receipt of the letter and the final confirmation of something he has already worked out – that Alex and her mother stole his money. We think his lack of a strong emotional response is possibly due to three separate things. Firstly, throughout this novel, he has shown remarkable resilience, fortitude and stoicism towards all the unpleasant events and experiences in his life – his mantra 'You can get used to anything after a while' is relevant here, and he has worked out long ago that Alex has betrayed him and stolen his money – the letter merely tells him where she is and what she is doing. Secondly, and there is less evidence for this in the text, it may be that Alex's betrayal of him and her theft of his money is softened somewhat by his obvious affection towards her: he may be pleased that she has the chance to achieve her dream – but he does not tell us this. Thirdly – and this ties in with Martyn's cynical, almost misanthropic view of human existence: Alex behaves just as everyone else that Martyn knows behaves; she acts completely selfishly with no thought or consideration for the effect on Martyn. Think about it: Martyn has been abandoned by his mother at an early age; his father abuses him verbally and physically; Dean tries to blackmail him; even Aunty Jean uses him in a way as a pawn or weapon in her conflict with Martyn's dad, her brother. So by abandoning him, betraying him and stealing his money, Alex is simply acting in the solipsistic way that almost every character in the novel acts. It is the sort of behaviour that Martyn has cynically come to expect from other people: they act in their own interests.

However, we think it can be argued that the novel ends on a positive note. The fact that it is starting to snow is significant, because earlier in the novel snow has been seen by Martyn as a purer, natural cleansing agent which makes his deprived and rundown area temporarily beautiful. Thus, it could be argued that Brooks is using the falling snow at the end of the novel to suggest that all the tangled events and messy betrayals of the past are things that Martyn can now put behind him. Snow, throughout the novel, has been associated with purity and cleanliness, and, therefore, hope for the future. The similarity with a detective story and its ending is clear: when one reads a detective story one has to know what happens, and now Martyn knows what has happened to Alex. The plot, the story, is complete and he can make sense of it.

There is another very positive aspect of the novel. Alex ends her letter by urging Martyn to carry on and write 'that murder mystery you told me about' – and in a strange sense he has. Of course, Kevin Brooks is the author of *Martyn Pig*, but if we accept the convention that Martyn is the narrator and tells us the story, then, in the fictional world of the novel, he has written a kind of mystery – and this trick is possible because of Brooks' choice of a first person narrator. In that sense, a completely fictional made-up sense, Martyn has achieved his ambition and written, through Brooks' imagination, the story of his father's death and the subsequent cover up, and his deception of the police.

This chapter is an effective ending to the novel. It
- brings closure by describing the funeral of Martyn's father and also describes how the police investigation peters out due to a lack of evidence;
- lets Martyn know exactly where Alex is and what she is doing;
- allows Martyn to live in a safe and quiet house which he clearly enjoys;
- ends on a very positive note.

Characters

Martyn

Some study guides may frame Martyn Pig as an unreliable narrator –

one who recounts the story from a biased perspective either through ignorance or self-interest. The story may open with a clearly delusional statement or slant, for instance, a person professing to be insane when their actions prove the opposite, or vice-versa. The unreliable narrator compromises his or her own credibility with the reader and the device is often used to provide a 'twist' at the end of the tale. However, the twist in *Martyn Pig* is Alex's elaborate manipulation of the situation to her own advantage and the shocking betrayal that this ultimately involves.

The phrase 'unreliable narrator' is a common one in literary criticism. As the phrase suggests it refers to a first person narrator who sees the events and characters of a novel so single-mindedly from his or her own point of view that we cannot trust them. A classic example would be Victor Frankenstein who narrates, either directly or indirectly, the novel *Frankenstein,* Nick Carraway the narrator of *The Great Gatsby,* or Pip in Charles Dickens' *Great Expectations*: all these characters are slightly delusional and biased, and see the events and other characters from their own self-centred point of view. So in *The Great Gatsby* Nick's admiration for Gatsby prevents him from admitting that Gatsby is simply a gangster involved in organized crime and killing people – not the romantic, heroic figure that Nick has presented him as.

We have come across some guides to *Martyn Pig* which suggest that Martyn is a simply an unreliable narrator – and cannot even accept that he is telling the truth about the way his father died, that he is covering something up or not telling the whole truth, so that he looks better. We would like to suggest that the truth is much more sophisticated and subtle than that.

Because Brooks is careful to construct a sympathetic character for Martyn, we believe Martyn completely in his account of how his Dad died. There is no reason to lie at all and, because Dad is also presented as a malign and abusive influence in Martyn's life, we felt no sympathy for Dad. In addition, in Brooks' presentation of Martyn, he has been so honest with the reader about so many things – his unhappiness, the teasing he has suffered about his name and his appearance, his unhappy and squalid home life and his feelings about his father ('I hated him.' p. 24), and his own low self-esteem – that the reader is inclined to believe him on the facts of his father's death.

Martyn is completely unaware of Alex's plot to murder Dean and to steal Martyn's money. He cannot tell the reader about something he is completely ignorant about. This is not being unreliable – it is better to think of Martyn as ingenuous – innocent, unknowing, unaware of Alex's manipulation of him.

However, I think it is possible to argue that there are areas of the novel where Martyn is too reticent about the truth or doesn't tell the whole truth. For example, he is clearly very attracted to Alex, but never really goes into detail or even admits that he has a strong sexual attraction for her. This is only unusual because he is so open about so many other things. At the same time, his feelings about his missing mother are never really explored – it seems that her abandonment of him has had no effect on him, or perhaps that Martyn's natural resilience and stoicism ('You can get used to just about anything given enough time.' p. 9) means that he can stifle any feelings he has about his mother. His affection for Alex remains after he realizes the truth about what she has done, and, in his accepting forgiveness of her, it is possible to see a little unreliability in Martyn's opinion. In the 'Epilogue' when he receives Alex's letter from America he expresses no anger or distress at what she has done. As readers we would do well to remember that Alex is not only a thief – she is a murderer. Perhaps Martyn's sense of morality is limited.

The character, Martyn, is clearly disadvantaged in life; his mother left when he was young and he lives an isolated life with his alcoholic, idle and abusive father. The only other adult in his life is his aunt, whom he dislikes greatly. On page 10 Martyn addresses the reader with: 'Think of the worst person you know, then double it, and you'll be half way to describing Aunty Jean...' He has no friends aside from Alex and is the subject of ridicule because of his name. In the opening chapter he speaks with an honest voice, one that elicits the reader's compassion. Describing the impact his name has on him, Martyn confesses:

Every time I had to tell someone my name I'd start to feel ill. Physically ill. Sweaty hands, the shakes, bellyache. I lived for years with the constant dread of having to announce myself (p. 8).

Martyn's interior monologue is peppered throughout the story and it is generally intelligent, gentle and transparent. However, whilst Martyn is not in our opinion an unreliable narrator he is the only voice within the novel. As such all the other characters are described in terms of what he sees and knows.

We can deduce from the information given on page 19 that Martyn, our protagonist, is 15 years' old; he talks about when he met Alex and how old he was at the time. As mentioned above Martyn, on the whole, is a gentle and intelligent boy. However, he is also prone to compulsive behaviour – he ritualistically cleans the house, at odds with the familiar, albeit stereotyped, notion of a teenage boy. His bedroom is stripped back and virtually bare: 'My room was like a palace compared to Dad's. Clean and white and odourless.' (p.82) He also washes himself in the same compulsive way: 'I went into the kitchen and washed up my plate and cup, turned off the light, locked the doors, and went upstairs. Peed again, washed again, cleaned my teeth again...' (p. 98). Later he explains the effect that a lack of cleanliness has on him:

Back home I tidied up. Without Dad around, the place was easy to keep clean. I used to hate the mess he made. Stuff all over the floor, dirty plates and cups... it was a tip. A never ending supply of rubbish. I couldn't stand it. All that jumble and dirt, it made me so I couldn't think straight. I need to see clean surfaces, flat and uncluttered. I need to see the true shape of things, the lines, the angles. Mess messes me up (p. 155-156).

Martyn's thinking returns again and again to the inevitability of life and his powerlessness to control it. Perhaps the author has chosen the cleaning compulsion to demonstrate the character's need to be in control of something. His immediate unkempt surroundings would provide the obvious opportunity.

On the matter of inevitability Martyn often refers to a quotation taken from Albert Einstein:

Everything is determined, he said, the beginning as well as the end, by forces over which we have no control. It is determined for the insect as well as for the star. Human beings, vegetables or cosmic dust, we all dance to a mysterious tune, intoned in the distance by an invisible piper (p. 49-50).

The invisible piper recurs several times in the story as Martyn daydreams about fate and determinism and while he ponders life the author often places him behind a window looking out on the world. This serves to highlight the limitations of his life – it is almost as if he is a caged bird surveying a world in which he plays no role. He certainly has a very negative opinion of that world and repeatedly describes his local surroundings as 'grey' and 'dull':

This house, this place where I lived, this street, this town; I hated it. Dirty-grey. Dark and cold, everything too close. All the people living in dull acceptance of their misery, their drab surroundings. I hate it (p.58).

It would seem that Martyn would much prefer to indulge his passion for murder-mysteries than partake of society. Alex is the clear exception. However, despite allowing Alex into his world, Martyn is an independent young man, probably born of neglect and the need to look after himself and his father. Their roles, prior to the incident, are reversed. Martyn feeds his father, does the shopping, cleans the house – all the roles usually associated with the adult of the house, not the child. Similarly, on page 11 we learn that Martyn has taken the initiative to complete a first aid course in order that he could: '...tell whether he (his dad) was dead or just dead drunk.' Martyn's self-sufficiency is demonstrated again on page 44 when he rejects Alex's invitation for him to stay at her house.

Martyn's love of words is demonstrated not only by his avid reading, but the way in which he plays with words, often to very comic effect: 'Sugar? Grain? Molasses? What *are* molasses? Mole asses. Mole arses. A boat full of moles' arses' (p. 103) and again on page 106: 'The sky's the limit. Pie in the sky. Steak and kidney pie. Snake and pygmy pie. Sky diver. Skyscraper...' However, his use of words occasionally verges on the old-fashioned which could be suggestive of a child who has had greater contact with adults than with his contemporaries. Notice the use of simile and idiom on page 156: 'happy as a clam...clean as a whistle...spick and span.' His choice of words here are quite archaic, indicative of an older generation.

The protagonist's relationship with Alex is unique. He has a tendency to be scathing of other people without truly knowing their individual stories. Aside from his father and aunt, notice how he describes the family on page 99: '...the young couple from next door slouched out dragging their snotty-nosed kids across the street. The father flicked a dead cigarette into the gutter, adjusted the bright Santa hat perched ridiculously on top of his head...' He also displays contempt when he recounts his journey to the beach with his former school 'friend': 'He wasn't a friend really, just someone I hung around with for a while. I never liked him... always had a bunged up nose...' (p. 103). Similarly, when he first encounters Peter Bennett, the Social Worker, he launches into a description bordering on cruel:

He was a weedy-looking young man with short ginger hair and a short ginger moustache that was hardly worth the bother of growing. It looked like a short ginger caterpillar...he looked like a bell ringer. His skin was sickly and colourless and his lips were too thin... (p. 201).

This default disapproval of others and his scathing descriptions serve to highlight just how special Alex is to him. He watches Alex and shares with the reader detailed descriptions of all the nuances particular to her. Throughout he is effusive and clearly besotted with Alex ('I could watch her forever' p. 151) before he finally comes to the realization that she is his adversary, the antagonist. Equally, his default disapproval of others, such as the social worker who is there in a supportive role, indicates a distrust of others, in particular adults.

Alex

Alex is without doubt, after Martyn, the most important character in the novel. Brooks uses her a device to further the plot and to resolve it as well. However, because she is Martyn's best friend and the story is told from Martyn's perspective, we never really see the true Alex and the role that she plays until Martyn himself works out what she has done. Prior to his realization that she has stolen his money and murdered Dean, Alex is Martyn's best and only friend and his sole confidante. He trusts her completely, and her betrayal of him by stealing his money is traumatic for Martyn.

It is no exaggeration to say that without Alex's involvement the plot could not have happened, and in this sense Brooks uses her as a plot device: without Alex and her access to her mother's car, Martyn would have no way to move his father's dead body. Without Alex's key to Dean's flat, Martyn would have no way of planting clues there which implicate Dean in Dad's death.

Martyn has known Alex for about two years after she and her mother moved in to a house across the road from Martyn. It is clear from his description of her that he is attracted to her:

I remember thinking to myself how nice she looked. Nice. She looked nice. Pretty. Kind of scruffy, with straggly black hair sticking out from a shapeless black hat. She wore battered old jeans and a long red jumper. I liked the way she walked too. An easy lope. (p. 19)

However, Alex is two years older than Martyn and he dismisses any thoughts of romance between them as 'a ridiculous idea' (p. 19). Nonetheless, throughout the novel Martyn often expresses his affection for Alex and the events they go through together – moving his Dad's corpse, Aunty Jean's visit, the disposal of the corpse in the gravel pit, the attempted blackmail by Dean – <u>appear</u> to bring them closer together.

It is important to note, however, that Martyn's feelings for Alex are always, to a certain extent, ambivalent:

When she smiled I'd sometimes get this sick feeling in my stomach, like...I don't know what it was like. One of those feelings when you don't know if it's good or if it's bad. One of those. (p. 17)

When Martyn tells us this early in the novel he clearly has in mind his mixed feelings of attraction to her – mixed because she is older and unattainable – however, when we reach the end of the novel and understand the depths of Alex's evil and treachery, we realize that in another sense he is right to be undecided about whether she is good or bad. She is good in the way she helps Martyn cover up his part in his father's death and in the way she frames Dean for the death; she is bad because she knowingly sends Dean to his death by cutting the brake cables and in the way she conspires with her mother to steal Martyn's money.

Alex's relationship with Dean is a problem. It is a problem because as readers, we could not see why a young woman as nice as Alex appears to be with such a person as Dean who is presented through Martyn's narration as so obnoxious and repellent. Martyn says of their relationship: 'It was just wrong....It stank. It was wrong for her to spend time with him. It was a waste. He was nothing. It was wrong. Wrong. Wrong. Wrong. She was too good for him' (pp. 22 -23).

The conclusion we came to is that Alex is with Dean for purely selfish reasons: Dean has a job (and therefore money), and he has his own transport and a flat. Therefore, as a boyfriend he has distinct advantages above Martyn – quite apart from the fact that Martyn is younger than Alex. Alex is presented as having no deep feelings for

Dean – she is prepared to tamper with his motorcycle brakes which leads directly to his death.

In some ways her relationship with Martyn is natural: they are near neighbours and are both in single-parent families; their fathers both drink heavily. But there are differences: Alex's mother works and was once well-known because of a television acting role; Martyn's Dad, it seems, has never worked in his life.

Apart from being vital to the plot of the novel, Alex is also used by Brooks to bring about the twist at the very end. Martyn may protect her because he still feels affection for her, but as readers we can see that Alex is cold, manipulative and evil – she kills Dean and steals from Martyn. Looking back at her role in the novel as a whole, we might wonder exactly when she took the decision to cheat Martyn – probably by the Friday, as she spends so much time upstairs while they are waiting for Aunty Jean to arrive. Martyn may be infatuated with her, but all the examples of prolepsis are connected with Alex and we might also wonder if there is anything at all she says which is true and sincere. Brooks is keen, through Martyn's narration, to show what a good actress she is: the first time she imitated Martyn's Dad, Martyn was convinced it was really his Dad speaking to him. It may even have been Alex who made the anonymous phone call to tip the police off about the whereabouts of the money.

Alex is completely unscrupulous in her manipulation of Martyn – and it is made slightly worse because she knows that he trusts her completely. He even tells her about his plans for what they could do together with the money – yet she still betrays him.

Dad

We only see Dad, Billy Pig, through Martyn's eyes and the words that Brooks uses, and Martyn makes no secret of his hatred for his father. There is a lot to hate. Billy Pig (only called 'William' by his fussy and interfering sister, Martyn's Aunty Jean) is an unemployed drunkard who spends every day and all evening drinking. In addition, he virtually chain-smokes and has a poor sense of personal hygiene.

Ironically William Pig knows how to behave as is shown by his behaviour prior to the court case which is to determine whether he or Aunty Jean has custody of Martyn, and in the few days preceding Aunty Jean's annual Christmas visit: he stops drinking; he shaves and bathes regularly; he wears a suit and tie in the house; he also treats Martyn with a certain degree of civility. All this demonstrates that he knows how a proper father should act, but as soon as the court case is settled and once Aunty Jean's visits are over, he quickly returns to his old ways and remains drunk, unshaven and unkempt every day.

Martyn's Mum

Martyn's mum, we learn on the opening page of the novel, has left Martyn and his father in the distant past and is hardly ever mentioned by Martyn: she is described as 'long since gone' by the time he was ten or eleven (p. 25). Aunty Jean implies that she left because of Dad's drinking. Martyn tell us that Aunty Jean 'blamed him for the divorce and everything, said that he'd driven Mum to the 'brink of despair'' (p. 11) – but that is only her opinion and there is no other evidence to support this, although married life with the drunken, aggressive and lazy Dad cannot have been easy. Aunty Jean's view is given extra credence when we discover that Alex's Mum left Alex's father for the same reason. But Alex's Mum took Alex with her; Martyn's Mum left him with Dad – and we are never told why, but to be rejected by your own mother must surely affect your sense of self-esteem.

What is perhaps more interesting is that Martyn, in all his long digressions, never once refers to his mother, and, from the evidence in the novel, has no contact with her. Martyn tells us a lot about the cheap and tawdry Christmas traditions in his house, but there is no mention of a card or a present from his mother. On the one hand, this creates sympathy for Martyn – abandoned by a mother who does not bother even to acknowledge his existence. On the other, it helps to explain –

along with many other things – Martyn's cynical, disillusioned view of life and the world. He reveals no emotions at all about his abandonment by his mother and, as he says in a different context, 'You can get used to just about anything given enough time' (p. 9). Although Martyn accepts his mother's abandonment with apparent stoicism, it could be argued that her departure and the fact that he has no contact with her has contributed significantly to his cynicism and lack of self-esteem. There is an interesting moment on page 45 when Martyn watches Alex going home to: 'her home, <u>her mother</u>, her warm bed' which hints that he perhaps misses his mother more than he admits (our underlining).

Alex's Mum

Alex's mum is an indistinct figure, in a sense. In the beginning we learn very little about her aside from a vague potted history provided by Alex. We are led to believe that she became a single parent as Alex's father was also a drunkard. She had been an actress, albeit not a particularly memorable one, starring in a day-time soap until her character got killed off. With financial pressures and jobs few and far between she supplements her income with nursing (Alex: 'she hates it' p.27). We know that Alex is proud of her mother and wants to follow in her footsteps as an actress, something which her mum was initially resistant to, but then to which she offered her full support (p.28).

On her physical appearance Martyn's description is equally vague and contradictory:

She was quite tall, for a woman. Sort of dumpy, too. Medium-tall and dumpy... her hair was black, like Alex's, but short... her face was grey and tired-looking... she wore faded dungarees and a black T-shirt, long beady earrings, and bracelets on her wrists... (p. 20).

If anything can be derived from this it would appear, from her choice of attire and preferred career, that she is quite a bohemian character and socially unconventional.

When Alex breaks the vase, Martyn is surprised by her mum's response; he anticipated anger but 'they just stood there giggling and hooting like a couple of mad people.' (p. 19) Martyn adds: 'Dad would have screamed blue murder and thumped me on the back of the head.' (p. 19). From this we are lead to believe that Alex's mum is a gentle woman and yet as the story unfolds she is implicated as a manipulative and opportunistic character.

Proleptic irony, which is peppered through the novel, arises as Alex describes her mother's talents: 'She's brilliant, Martyn, you ought to see her. She's only got to raise an eyebrow and she becomes a different person...' Although we never really find out who masqueraded as Martyn's father, both at the bank and in the anonymous phone call tipping Breece off, all the indications point towards her. The fact that her acting career ended when her character, Shirley Tucker and Shirley's boyfriend were *'tragically killed* in a motorcycle accident.' (p.27) again suggests that Alex's mum played a significant part in the events to unfold. (It is interesting that the author has italicized the *'tragically* killed' as if to emphasize the irony of the 'coincidental' deaths). Did this give her the knowledge required to instruct Alex how to tamper with the brakes? Martyn later reflects on the circumstances surrounding Dean's death: 'No, I thought. It's not real. Severed brake lines? Not in real life. That's the kind of thing that only happens in novels. It's ridiculous.' (p.186). Here Martyn's opinion highlights the connection between the fictional and factual deaths and suggests that the two are intractably linked and as the story unfolds so too does Alex's mum's apparent collusion.

Aunty Jean

Aunty Jean is Martyn's father's older sister. She is described through the words of Martyn as a 'terrible woman'. On page 10 Martyn's contempt and loathing is palpable:

Think of the worst person you know, then double it, and you'll be half way to Aunty Jean. I can hardly bear to describe her, to tell you the truth. Furious is the first word that comes to mind. Mad, ugly and furious. An angular woman, cold and hard, with crispy blue hair and a face that makes you shudder.

He continues:

I don't know what colour her eyes are, but they look as if they never close. They have about as much warmth as two depthless pools. Her mouth is thin and pillar-box red, like something drawn by a disturbed child. And she walks faster than most people run. She moves like a huntress, quick and quiet, homing in on her prey...

Aunty Jean is clearly a woman whose demeanour incites fear in others. The author uses anthropomorphism to reinforce this on page 85: 'I could tell it was Aunty Jean by the tone of the bell. It sounded terrified.'

At the start of the novel we learn that Aunty Jean had unsuccessfully sought custody of Martyn, but Martyn did not consider this an act of altruism - just a means of getting one up on his father: 'She didn't give a hoot for my innocent life, she just wanted to kick Dad while he was down, kick him where it hurts...She despised him as much as he despised her...' (p. 11). Aunty Jean's rationale for applying for custody is Martyn's father's alcoholism; however, later in the novel we learn that she too is an alcoholic, albeit not a violent one, and therefore has a hypocritical trait:

The funny thing is, it turns out she's a drinker too. Just like Dad...She makes out she only drinks socially – sherry, cocktails, that kind of thing – but she's bottles hidden all over the place (p. 212).

However, despite Martyn's patent dislike for his aunt, once she has custody of him, she does seek to better him and seems to have genuine concerns over his education: 'She's forever trying to *educate* me...constantly introducing me to what she thinks are the social niceties of life – boring little parties, nice people, manners, hobbies...' (p. 212) In the Epilogue Martyn himself confesses that things are not quite as a bad as he had anticipated: 'I've been at Aunty Jean's for a year now. It's not as bad as I thought it would be' (p. 212). In conclusion Aunty Jean is not the monster initially portrayed by Martyn as she does demonstrate compassion towards him – in this sense she stands alone amongst the adults in Martyn's life as the only singular individual to protect and nurture him.

In this new living arrangement and, for the first time, the author allows Martyn to cast aside his bleak descriptions of his immediate vicinity: 'Spring sunshine flooded in through the open conservatory doors, a smell of fresh flowers breezed in the air.' (p. 216). This reinforces Aunty Jean as a force for good.

Detective Inspector Breece

Through Brooks' novel, Breece joins the list of fictional detectives that Martyn through his reading and watching of detective series on television is already familiar with. Martyn first meets him late on Tuesday evening when the police call at his house to question him. Breece, the Detective Inspector, speaks first and this is our first impression of him through Martyn's eyes:

…a silver-haired man with a weathered face and sharp eyes. Medium height, stout, round-shouldered. He had a crumpled look about him. Beneath his raincoat he wore a dark blue suit that didn't seem to fit properly. (p. 181)

Later we learn that Breece walks with a 'slight limp' (p. 184). Having said that they want to talk to Martyn about his father, Breece asks Martyn how well he knows Dean West, while Detective Sergeant Finlay goes upstairs to use the lavatory. In fact, Breece controls the entire scene, bombarding Martyn with questions which become remorseless. Detective Finlay has found oil on a flannel in the bathroom and calls Breece out of the kitchen to show him, but Martyn is unaware of this.

Breece also produces the letters from the solicitor to Martyn's father which Alex had planted at Dean's flat – but he also produces the piece of paper on which Martyn had demonstrated to Alex his ability to forge his Dad's signature and which Martyn had thought that Alex had thrown away. As he does so, Martyn notes that Breece's 'pale blue eyes drilled into mine, unblinking' (p. 185). Breece then reveals that Dean died the day before in a road accident with a bus after his brake lines had been intentionally severed. At this point Breece produces from his pocket a plastic bag that Finlay has put the flannel in – it seems that the police think that Martyn cut Dean's brake cables and wiped his hand on the flannel. Breece comes out with a flurry of questions until stopped by Finlay: the police can only interview a minor (someone under 16) if another adult is present. Breece calms down and tells Martyn to get his coat and asks Finlay to call Social Services. Martyn is being taken to the police station to be questioned in the presence of a social worker.

In the police car Martyn tells us that Breece 'just sat there rigidly with his arms crossed, staring out at the rain. Fed up, probably. Working late. Christmas Eve' (p. 187) and later, when it turns out that no one from social services is available and the police will have to wait until the next day to question Martyn properly, Breece looks 'tired and irritated' (pp. 188 – 189).

On Christmas Day Breece informs Martyn that they have found the dead body of his father as they received an anonymous phone call in the early hours of the morning about the location of the body and police divers have been to the quarry to retrieve the body. When he tells Martyn this, Breece stares at Martyn when he delivers this information, keen to ascertain whether Martyn shows any guilt in his reaction. Breece says 'I'm sorry', but Martyn comments '…there was no sorrow in his eyes, just a world-weary suspicion' (p. 195). As the female police officer comforts Martyn (who has started crying), Breece continues to stare at him with 'cold, hard eyes' (p. 195). Breece is presented as Martyn's antagonist in this chapter, but as readers we can see that he has two murders to solve and simply wants to find out the truth – just as Martyn has struggled during the night to come to terms with what Alex has done.

During the interview with Martyn, Breece continues to ask searching questions which Martyn evades by telling lies and concocting a false story to explain his connection with Dean. It is interesting that in this long passage Martyn and Breece share a contempt and disdain for Peter Bennett, the social worker. Breece dislikes him because he interferes in the questioning in his well-meaning attempt to shield Martyn from unfair questions; ironically, Martyn despises him for being so patronizing and condescending. In the end they let Martyn go unwillingly to his Aunty Jean's, because they have no evidence that he had anything to do with either death. However, Martyn is intelligent in that he knows Breece still has strong suspicions about him:

Breece was watching me from across the room. I knew he didn't believe me. He knew I was lying. And I knew he didn't know why. But what could he do? (p. 209)

Breece visits Martyn frequently at his Aunty Jean's house to ask him further questions about the case which shows that he retains his suspicions about Martyn's involvement. However, Martyn sticks to his original story and Breece has not got enough evidence to penetrate Martyn's lies. As Martyn notes, 'He knew I had *something* to do with it, but he couldn't work out what' (p. 214). Martyn thinks that Breece thinks that Dean killed Martyn's Dad and that Martyn cut the cables of Dean's motorbike's brakes – but he has no proof. On his final visit Martyn describes him as 'looking wearier than ever. Same old worn-out suit, same old worn-out face' (p. 216). Then he surprises Martyn by mentioning Alex for the first time: the police have been checking the phone records and noticed that Alex and Martyn spoke to each other a lot on the phone around the time of the murders. Again Martyn lies to the police to protect Alex, but Breece is unconvinced of Martyn's own innocence, asking him, just before he leaves, how it feels to have got away with murder. When Martyn says he does not know, Breece replies, 'No…I don't suppose you do' (p. 218) and he smiles for the very first time. Martyn's involvement with the police ends enigmatically.

Martyn attributes Breece's irritability on the night of Christmas Eve to the season and the late hour. It is may also be caused by frustration at having to wait to question Martyn and also the daily contact with criminals and criminality. In addition, when he sees Martyn on Christmas Day he has not shaved, is wearing the same suit and smells of 'sweat and tired whisky' (p. 194). It is not unusual in modern detective fiction for the main detective to be psychologically tired and damaged by a life spent investigating human evil – which arguably is what causes crime. In addition, several modern fictional detectives drink heavily or have battled with alcohol in the past. We think that may account for the way Brooks has presented Breece – tired, slightly disheveled, yet despite his instinct that tells him Martyn had something to do with both Dad's and Dean's deaths, he cannot prove a thing. This instinct is also typical of many fictional detectives. Wearing the same suit and failing to shave are meant to indicate an obsession with the work of a policeman and of being too preoccupied with police work to worry about such things.

Detective Sergeant Finlay

Detective Sergeant Finlay, whose role is minimal within the novel and appears towards the conclusion, is introduced to Martyn on page 182 by Detective Inspector Breece when the two policeman visit Martyn's home. Martyn immediately adopts his standard reproachful response to new people describing Finlay as: 'Tall, sad-faced, about thirty, he looked a bit dim but probably wasn't.'

Together, Finlay and Breece fulfill a very particular function, they are the Morse and Lewis of Martyn's story. Finlay, the underdog, quietly undertakes the menial aspects of the investigation – making the call to social services, pushing the buttons on the tape recorder, driving the car and taking notes whilst Breece asks the penetrating questions. This hierarchical arrangement and double act is a familiar one in police fiction and film and in this sense their relationship is somewhat of a cliché but a fitting one for this murder-mystery.

WPC Sally Saunders

On Christmas Day (p. 194) Martyn is introduced to WPC Sally Saunders. Martyn describes her as 'younger, prettier (than the policewoman from the night before), with pale blonde hair and a kind face.' Martyn contrasts the smell of Breece ('sweat and tired whisky' p. 194) with the policewoman's: 'I couldn't help noticing the sweet smell of her perfume – so sweet it was almost sickly. But not unpleasant. It reminded me of the scent that the girls in the first year at school wear – cheap sweets and flowers (p. 195).' The contrast serves to highlight Martyn's inherent dislike of Breece and conversely his fondness for the policewoman. Similarly, Martyn familiarly refers to the policewoman by her first name, Sally, while he adopts the policeman's surname devoid of his official title of Detective Inspector.

Sally is clearly an empathetic and non-judgemental character, which is displayed in the softness of her voice and the physical contact she has with Martyn: '...she sat down and put her arm around my shoulder.' (p.195). Unlike the policemen she does not challenge Martyn, just offers comfort and tea.

Peter Bennett

Social Worker, Peter Bennett, is drafted into the police interview on account of Martyn's age. His role is to support, guide and guard Martyn as a legal minor. Martyn's response to him is scathing, despite the fact that the Social Worker is there to protect him: '...he looked like a bell-ringer. His skin was sickly and colourless and his lips were too thin. He looked as if he didn't eat properly.' (p. 201). While he counsels Martyn on what to expect in the interview and reassures him that he is not under arrest Martyn's dislike intensifies: 'you don't have to answer any of the questions, blah blah blah – but his voice was too boring to listen to and I found myself staring at his clothes...' (p. 201).

Despite Martyn's scorn, Peter Bennett seems genuinely concerned with Martyn's welfare and becomes incensed at the line of questioning.

When Breece describes the recovery of Martyn's father's body, Peter Bennett becomes animated in his objections: "Inspector...' Bennett piped up in his for-goodness-sake-this-is a child-you're-talking-to voice.' When Breece ignores Peter Bennett's protestations and continues to talk vividly about the water-filled quarry, the Social Worker again defends Martyn: "'Really Inspector!' Bennett snapped as he jumped up out his chair. 'I can't allow this!'" (p. 203).

Throughout the interview Peter Bennett clearly has Martyn's best interests at heart. However, Martyn seems incapable of identifying this humanity and when told that he will need to stay with his aunt he launches into a caustic diatribe: 'His stupid voice, the way he talked to me like I was mental or something. I felt like punching him in the mouth. I knew I would if this carried on much longer.' (p.209). Peter Bennett's role, thus, tells us rather more about Martyn than about himself. Martyn is compelled towards the violence that he abhors and has suffered at the hands of his father when his independence and vision for the future is vetoed.

Language and Style

We have come across many students views, eyes glaze over when the words language and style are mentioned – not to mention form and structure. However, Assessment Objectives Two, which we cover in the model answers section, requires you to include in your answer some comments about language, structure and form. There is no need to be intimidated by these terms. They can be hard to write about effectively, but they are fairly easy to grasp and understand.

Think of it this way: Martyn, Martyn's Dad, Alex – all the characters – are not real people. They exist only through words – the words that Brooks has used to present them with or describe them or allowed them to say. Let us take a simple example: on page 23 Martyn returns home with the Christmas shopping and Brooks writes 'the rain was turning to sleet as I pushed open the back gate... stepping over dog turds and squashed cigarette ends and bin-liners full of empty beer cans'. When we study a work of literature, we must assume that every single word, every change of paragraph and even every italicized word has been carefully chosen by the author. Now imagine how different an impression we would have got if, when Martyn returns home with the shopping on page 23, Brooks had written instead 'A bright ray of sunlight beamed through the clouds and I pushed open the new back gate and walked to the back door across the freshly-swept patio': It is not enough to say – well, Martyn's home is not like that. It is like that because Brooks has chosen everything that happens in the novel and every word; Brooks has decided that Martyn's home should be as it is.

A crucial factor affecting the book's style is Brooks' decision to tell the story in the first person from Martyn's point of view. This means that Brooks has to write in such a way that we, as readers, are convinced that the words that we are reading on the page could have come from the character that Brooks has created – a fifteen year old English boy from a poor background and with an abusive father.

So what techniques does Brooks use? They can be divided into two broad types: the ones he uses to give the impression of a speaking voice talking to us, and, secondly, those that are specific to Martyn Pig and his character.

1. Brooks uses single sentences as stand-alone paragraphs for emphasis and to highlight the importance of certain things. There are countless examples; 'I had to get out' (p.15); 'She never looked back' (p.18 and many more) ; 'It was raining' (p. 19'; on page 192 a whole string of them:

'I was ready to start thinking again.

How did it happen?

Why did it happen?

Who thought of it?

Was the whole thing Alex's idea?

Did her mum put her up to it?

Or was it a bit of both?'

Here on page 192 the stand-alone sentences reflect Martyn's slow turning over in his mind the various possibilities of how he has been betrayed, and they also draw attention to the important content of each sentence – attention which would be diffused if they were part of one long paragraph.

2. Brooks allows Martyn to use contractions – can't, don't, shouldn't – which are more common in speech and also make the style of the novel less formal.

3. Brooks allows Martyn to use swear words or taboo words: 'bloody' (now considered a mild swear word) and on one occasion the more offensive 'twat'. This helps the novel's sense of realism.

4. Brooks uses minor sentences a lot. Minor sentences are (technically) ungrammatical sentences, and they consist of a phrase or very often in *Martyn Pig* a single word. Their effect is two-fold: they help give the impression of a speaking voice, because when we speak we use minor sentences – odd phrases or single words - a great deal.

5. Brooks allows Martyn to address the reader directly: 'I know what you're thinking. Why didn't I call 999, call out the emergency services?' (p. 38) and in this paragraph Brooks even allows Martyn to speak for the readers, as it were, as he imagines the questions we might ask of him: 'Why didn't you give him artificial respiration? You studied first aid, didn't you? Why didn't you try to save his life?' (p.38).This technique helps to bring the character closer to the reader so that our relationship with the fictional Martyn is more intimate and we

are more likely to sympathize and empathize with him. This is crucial in our assessment of his relationship with his Dad: 'You would have hated him, too, if you'd ever met him' (p.24).

So far all these techniques could be applied to any first-person teenage narrator, but Brooks also uses other techniques to give Martyn a distinctive and individual voice and to encourage the reader to see that voice as authentic and engaging:

1. There are short passages where Brooks repeats through Martyn's voice certain words: a good example is in the first chapter on page 19 when Martyn watches Alex and her mother when they first move in and Brooks starts almost every sentence with 'I watched her....'

2. Brooks allows Martyn to use original and striking similes:

   'Pounding, pounding rain. Louder and louder like a thousand angry fingers rapping on the window' (p. 63);

   'Her hair sat on top of her head like a blue Brillo pad' (p. 86);

   'The pores of her skin were stained, like small blue stars' (p. 87);

   'It sounded like the dying groans of a sea monster' (p. 90);

   'The snow was already starting to melt on the road, oozing into the gutters like mashed potato swimming in gravy' (p. 110).

   These similes are striking and original in their own right, but because they are, as it were, attributed to Martyn, the reader is drawn to greater empathy with him because of his perceived verbal dexterity.

3. Because the novel is set in winter and because of the poor area that Martyn lives in, Brooks frequently uses the word 'dead' – not simply in relation to Martyn's Dad and Dean (who are both

literally dead by the end of the novel). The weather and the area around Martyn's house are often described as dead which reinforces the novel's central events and which also suggests Martyn's deep pessimism. For example, on page 99 the morning is personified – it 'arrived cold, dull and heavy' – and in the same paragraph the day is described as 'dead green', the weeds outside the house are 'dead green spikes', and a neighbor flicks a 'dead cigarette' into the gutter.

4. Brooks allows Martyn to have short passages of the novel where he indulges in free association with words – usually to reflect the rapidity of Martyn's thoughts and their essential humour:

A long container ship….Where was it going? What was it carrying? Sugar? Grain? Molasses? What are molasses? Mole asses. Mole arses. A boat full of moles' arses (p. 103);

Every snowflake is unique. Is it? How can you tell?….Who knows? Snow. Snowball. Snowdrop. Drop of snow. Snowgoose. That's no goose, that's my wife. Snowshoe. Bless you. Snowman. Walking in the air. Abominable. Snow. Snow. Quick, quick snow (p. 106);

Sea. Seashell. Michelle. Seashore. Seasick. Sea-slug. Seaweed. Sea-dog. Salty sea-dog, har har. Seaplane. Sea-Scout. See you later, alligator. Sea anemone. See an enemy. What else? The sky. Hell, I don't know what the sky is. The sky's just the sky. The sky's the limit. Pie in the sky. Steak and kidney pie. Snake and pygmy pie. Sky diver. Skyscraper. Sky rocket. Sky lark. Sky piper. Sea-piper. Invisible piper (p. 106)

These quotations are all taken from Martyn's visit to the beach. They demonstrate his wit, his quick thinking and his intelligence, and they help endear him to us.

Another major part of the style – which does come out in words and phrases and which we have mentioned in the commentaries in each chapter – is Brooks's use of prolepsis. At the end of the novel, when we know all the facts of what happens or, if we read the novel for a second time, many things are filled with proleptic irony: every time Alex walks away from Martyn without looking back; every time Alex's acting skills are mentioned or praised by Martyn; every time Martyn expresses gratitude or wonder at how Alex is helping him – all these things become ironic when we look back because they are so far from the truth.

Setting

The novel is set in a town in southern England which is twelve miles from the sea – given Martyn's bus trip to the beach. Brooks does not specify the location, but the way he renders the speech of the market stall holders in the first chapter suggests that the town is in the south: 'Getchur luvverly turkeys 'ere!... Plenny a luvverly turkeys!... Wrapping papah! Ten sheets a paand!' (p. 16). Here the spelling of stall holders' words (designed to imitate their accents) indicate a setting somewhere in the south of England.

What is more important in the novel as a whole is that Brooks uses various settings to reflect Martyn's mood or state of mind, and to emphasize certain facts about his life or his emotional state. It is possible to make a clear distinction between places where Martyn feels at ease and comfortable – and there are very few such places in the novel – and places that he does not like or feels uncomfortable in.

At the end of the novel Martyn feels safe and comfortable at Aunty Jean's house – in large part because it is clean and ordered. In a very important passage in the novel he tells us that now that his Dad is dead:

...the place was easy to keep clean. I used to hate the mess he made. Stuff all over the floor, dirty plates and cups... it was a tip. A never ending supply of rubbish. I couldn't stand it. All that jumble and dirt, it made me so I couldn't think straight. I need to see clean surfaces, flat and uncluttered. I need to see the true shape of

things, the lines, the angles. Mess messes me up (p. 155-156).

This need to 'see the true shape of things' may explain his liking for detective stories – after all, in detective novels, the leading detective often makes sense of a seemingly random and chaotic series of events surrounding a murder and solves the case by discovering who the murderer is.

The general setting is Martyn's house – a generally squalid little house in a working class area of a poor town. Martyn expresses contempt for the people who live there and he feels constrained by his immediate environment:

This house, this place where I lived, this street, this town; I hated it. Dirty-grey. Dark and cold, everything too close. All the people living in dull acceptance of their misery, their drab surroundings. I hated it. (p. 58)

Essentially all the places in the novel can be categorized according to how Martyn feels about them. The ones he dislikes – Dad's room, the living room, his own part of town, the town centre, the Bargain Bin shop – are smelly or noisy or generally in need of care and refurbishment or redecoration. The places he likes the most – his own room, Aunty Jean's house and, paradoxically, the police station – are clean and orderly, and afford him enough silence to enable him to think.

When he thinks he will have £30,000 to spend as he likes, Martyn fantasizes about going to remote places with Alex as his companion:

I could buy a small island. Right out in the middle of the sea where no one else could get to. We could live there, make friends with the animals, build a little cabin, spend all day talking, walking on the beach. ....or we could go to Australia, or America, find some remote place out in the desert where Indians used to live. The badlands, miles and miles of nothing.... (p. 96 – 97)

These fantasies based on getting the money inherited by his dead father help demonstrate what Martyn dislikes about his current life – the noise and the people. His dream of buying a small island encapsulates perfectly his dislike of other people and his wish to be alone – so different from the real setting of the novel.

Themes

Loneliness and Alienation

Martyn, the novel's chief protagonist, is very lonely. He hates his Dad and his Aunty Jean – the two relatives that Brooks mentions in the text. He has not seen his mother for several years. Martyn never refers to friends or mates from school, and his only friend apparently is Alex – but by the end of the novel she has betrayed him and stolen his money. Even during his shopping expedition to the town centre in the opening chapter, he sees no one that he knows from school. It is fair to say that Martyn is a very lonely young man. Even his favourite pastime – reading detective stories – is a solitary activity. Apart from when he is with Alex or being interrogated by the police, Martyn spends a lot of time on his own. It is remarkable too that Martyn's characteristic relationship with other people is watching them: often in the course of the novel, he is looking out of a window, observing people from a distance and commenting, usually critically, on their appearance or behavior.

The section on Martyn's character above goes into detail about the poverty of the area that Martyn lives in. In Martyn's case he seems so distanced and so critical of the area he lives in and the whole town that he could be said to be alienated from other ordinary people. He simply does not like other people and has no respect for the way they behave.

Let us consider two important passages. In the first Martyn is looking out of his window and reflecting on the area he lives in and its inhabitants:

Look at this place. These squalid houses, dirty little streets, dead skies. Nothing. No life, no point. Too many people with nothing to say and nothing to do and nowhere to go. Grey souls. Waiting for it all to end. This is it, this is what I have…. Me, alone in a dirty little house, in a dirty little town. (pp. 95 – 96)

Martyn is truly alienated from his environment, and cynical and bitter here about the meaning of life and the aspirations of his fellow townsfolk. This, of course, is why the £30,000 is so important to him: it gives him the chance to escape his 'dirty little town' and live a better life.

However, it should be noted that Martyn seems to enjoy being alone. After Dad's death – apart from showing no deep emotional response, he also cleans the house and seems happy to cook for himself: he is self-contained, stoical and resilient. It is also interesting that his fantasies about what he will do with Alex and the £30,000 involve places that are remote and far from other people. He writes 'I could buy a small island. Right out in the middle of the sea where no one else could get to… or we could go to Australia, or America, find some remote place out in the desert' (pp. 96 – 97) Martyn's loneliness is a choice because he is so disillusioned with his current life and so contemptuous of other people.

Notions of Right and Wrong

The issue of what is right and what is wrong – morality – lies at the heart of the novel, and it is explicitly discussed by Martyn and Alex as they reflect on what they are doing or plan to do with Dad's body. Their conversations – and especially Martyn's pronouncements on the matter – suggest that morality is just an artificial social construct.

In the opening chapter, as soon as she hears about Dad's death, Alex urges Martyn to go to the police and she urges this course of action again on Thursday. Martyn is worried that the delay between his Dad's death and his reporting of it will cast suspicion on him. On Friday over tea, before moving Dad's corpse from the living room to his own bedroom, Alex asks, 'Are we bad?...Bad. Evil. Wrong' (p. 74). Martyn replies, 'It's a relative kind of thing, badness. Good, bad. Right, wrong.

What's the difference? Who decides?' (p. 74). Alex points out that what they have already done (failing to report a death) and what they are about to do at the weekend – move Dad's corpse and conceal it, without reporting the death - are against the law. She goes on to argue that certain crimes – such as rape and murder are always wrong - they are recognized as universally wrong in all human societies. However, Martyn adopts the extreme position of arguing that

Whatever any one does, it's not wrong to them.... It's only wrong if you think it's wrong. If you think it's right, and others think it's wrong, then it's only wrong if you get caught. (p. 76)

This is a very extreme position, because if Martyn really believed it, it could lead to social chaos and breakdown, and it is important to note that almost immediately Martyn says, 'I don't know. Maybe. Maybe not.' Much later in the novel when Martyn, in his room in the police station, finally and fully understands that Alex has killed Dean it should be noted that Martyn vomits copiously into the toilet: his instinctive reaction to the fact that Alex is a murderer suggests very strongly that he disagrees with his earlier pronouncement on morality: some crimes such as murder are always wrong. Indeed, in the paragraph following his spontaneous vomiting he comments: '...why did I feel so bad about Alex killing him? Why did it frighten me? What made it so *wrong*?' (p. 191). In the end, therefore, Martyn accepts that some things are morally wrong.

Of course, there are other actions and behaviour throughout the novel which we might see as wrong or immoral. It could be argued that Martyn is wrong to hide his father's body: he fails to report a death and wastes a lot of police time. Dad is wrong in the way he treats Martyn, although it is not illegal: he did break Martyn's wrist when Martyn was much younger, but Dad gets away with it because Martyn lies to the doctor and says he fell off his bike. It might even be argued that Martyn's Mum was wrong to leave him and have no contact with him – but we do not know enough about the circumstances or the details of her marriage to Billy Pig to judge. In order to protect himself, Martyn lies many times to the police – in order to distance himself from Dad's death and Dean's murder: Martyn shows no sense of guilt at these lies – for him they are simply a means of self-preservation.

Despite the affection Martyn still feels for her (he protects her from Breece in the 'Epilogue'), Alex is an immoral person who does not get caught: she is a liar, a thief and a murderer.

The Nature of Reality

Several times throughout the narrative, Martyn refers to his experience as a kind of waking up or a realization that 'reality' is different from life as portrayed in books/films or on television. Aspects of this experience that fall into this category for Martyn are experiences of being around death; of contemplating the difference between childhood fantasy and adult experience; and of being caught up in a murder investigation. There is also the reference, somewhat Biblical in origin, to Martyn's having given up childhood things. All these experiences, and Martyn's commentary on them, suggest that he is to some degree coming of age, realizing that the ways he had of interpreting the world had more to do with fantasy, and wishful thinking, than with the way things actually are. It is here, perhaps, that questions of Martyn's narrative reliability come into the equation.

It could also be argued, however, that thematic questions about the nature of reality are explored in another way from the angle that one's reality can be changed if one is prepared, as Martyn and Alex clearly are, to take some risks and make some bold, perhaps somewhat questionable, choices. Their present realities are constrictive and unhappy, and they become determined to do whatever it takes to change them. The narrative's third thematic consideration comes into play and its contemplation of the allure of freedom.

Incarceration, Confinement and the Allure of Freedom

It could be argued that the novel's central narrative line is defined less by the facts of the circumstances (i.e. Dad dying) and more to do with the prospect of freedom that those circumstances opens up. For Martyn, the prospect of freedom is immediate - freedom from violence and from other forms of abuse and when the prospect of money comes into the picture, freedom from everything that his life has both been and promises to remain. The money, in turn, also brings the prospect of freedom into Alex's life - specifically, the freedom for both her and her mother to pursue their longed-for careers as actresses. It could even be argued, in fact, that although the narrative never actually comes out and says it, Dean's attempt to blackmail his way into possession of that money represents an expression of a desire for freedom. It certainly is for the other two, so it stands to reason that it could also be so for Dean. In all three cases, the prospect of freedom, and its simultaneous allure, leads these three characters to do increasingly desperate, morally ambiguous things - it is, it seems, the driving need at the core of their identities, and therefore of their actions.

Meanwhile, it's important to note that the novel also contains contrasting experiences of a lack of freedom. Dad and, to a lesser degree, Jean and Breece, are both defined by the lack of freedom in their lives. Dad is trapped by his addictions, Jean is trapped by hers and her beliefs about morality, Breece is trapped by his job's necessity of responding only to facts (he believes Martyn is in some way guilty, but can't act on that belief because he is trapped by his job's insistence on basing guilt solely on evidence). In providing such a vivid contrast to the freedom envisioned and pursued by Martyn, Alex, and perhaps Dean, the experiences of Dad, Jean and Breece more vividly define the intensity of need and a lack of freedom.

It should also be noted that Martyn often spends much time reflecting on the world from behind a window. Even when he is finally re-homed with Auntie Jean this habit remains with him: '...she always wants to know where I'm going, where I've been...Not that it really matters, I hardly ever go anywhere...' (p. 212). In a sense, Martyn self-imposes incarceration on himself to avoid the world he considers with such disdain and distrust.

Sleep and Death

As befits this often darkly comedic book, the text is peppered with the words 'death', 'dying' and 'decay', particularly in relation to Martyn's immediate surroundings: 'I opened the bedroom curtains and gazed out at the colours of the day. Grey, brown. Brown, grey. Black. Dead green...Dead green spikes dropped with the weight of frost...The father flicked a dead cigarette...' (p. 99). As a reader the theme of death is made inescapable.

In the novel the protagonist is forced to confront death first hand; the character recalls the incident in which he deliberately killed a bird which left him '...cold. Ashamed. Scared. Dirty and bad.' (p. 150). However, later it is revealed that Martyn's response to his father's death conjures up no such feelings: 'Gone. I'd never see him again. I stared down at the big green nylon cocoon and wondered if I ought to feel something. Anything. But I didn't. There was nothing.'

Brooks presents Martyn as a character who considers death a finality. The exchange between Alex and Martyn on page 74 is revealing as Martyn rejects the notion of death as a form of sleeping:

'It's nothing to be scared of,' I said. 'Just imagine he's asleep.'
'Not dead, just sleeping.'
'What?'
'That's what it says on the gravestones – not dead, just sleeping.'
'A dirty trick,' I said.

Following the disposal of the body in the gravel pit, the character of Martyn again holds to this notion: 'Buried. Gone. Not sleeping, just dead.' (p. 131).

The theme of death is intertwined with the theme of sleeping. The protagonist's sleep and waking often punctuate the days within the book. 'Monday' provides a particularly revealing passage which is worth quoting in whole:

Sometimes I try to imagine what happens when I'm sleeping. You can never know, can you? You never see yourself asleep. You don't know what happens. You lose yourself. Every night, you lose yourself to an unknown world.

I imagine the structure of my body idling. Ticking over. The innards are at rest. I'm automatic. Electric things that work me continue to work, crackling in the dead dark of my head. I move, crawling blindly on knotted sheets, twitching. I talk to myself about things I don't understand and I watch talking pictures, broken images, rummages of life's rubbish. Dreams. The sleeping me. A self-cleansing organism, scrapping out the useless much of a mind. Washing up.

Clearly, the character considers sleep to be beneficial, a cleansing device to eliminate unnecessary or hurtful thoughts and images; a means of processing the details of the day. However, the reality is that sleep often brings disturbing dreams. 'Thursday' opens with Martyn dreaming of being interviewed by Inspector Morse on the charge of having shot his father. Martyn wakes 'screaming vainly into the darkness.' (p. 47).

On dreams Brooks provides Martyn with:

The thing about dreams, they don't come from anywhere else but yourself. It's not as if there's some evil demon waiting around somewhere, waiting for you to sleep so he can sneak into your mind and show you all his crazy things. It's you that does it. It's your mind. Whatever demons there are, you invite them in. They're your demons. No one else's (p. 47).

Martyn's attitude here seems typical of the resilient self-reliance he has shown throughout the novel. He seems in control of himself and his feelings – which is the way he likes things to be.

Model Answers

In English and English Literature it is impossible to write a 'model' answer, because there are countless ways to write a good answer that will achieve a high grade. As a subject, English thrives on different opinions and individual insights – your own personal response. However, through teaching we come across a lot of students who say, 'I have no idea how to start' or who have deep responses to a particular story but are unsure about how to put their ideas down on paper. So what follows are answers to questions asked by the exam board on *Martyn Pig* in 2011 and in 2012 – not perfect answers at all, but examples of what might have been written. If we have used words you do not understand, it is to encourage you to use them. There are some golden rules to remember when you write on literature: quote often, but keep your quotations short and always comment on them; answer the question and use the words that the examiner uses in the question; do not write about the characters as if they are real people – they are not – they are imaginary creations of the writer; try to show an awareness of other interpretations – if something in a story is unclear or capable of being interpreted in more than one way, have the confidence to say so – provided you are answering the question. We have tried to put this advice into practice in our writing of the model answers.

The questions at Foundation and Higher Tier do differ in each examination session, and they also differ in that Foundation Tier questions use slightly simpler language and bullet points. We, however, make no distinctions below between the two tiers as the structure of the questions is essentially the same, as are the assessment objectives. We have kept the answers that follow to between 500 and 900 words or a little more: they are not 'perfect' answers (such things do not exist in English Literature) and we could have written much, much more, but we are conscious that you have only a very limited amount of time to answer the question in the examination.

On the exam paper you have a choice of two questions: you answer only **one**.

It is worth remembering that although there are **four** assessment objectives in English Literature, but that in Section A of Unit One: Exploring Modern Texts where you will find the questions on *Martyn Pig*, you are only being assessed on two of the objectives:

- Assessment Objective One which asks you to 'respond to texts critically and imaginatively; select and evaluate relevant textual detail to illustrate and support interpretations'.

- Assessment Objective Two which asks you to 'explain how language, structure and form contribute to the writer's presentation of ideas, themes and settings'.

How do you respond to Dean in the novel *Martyn Pig*?

Write about:

- ### What you think about Dean from what he says and does

- ### The methods Brooks uses to present Dean

On page 21 our protagonist introduces Dean and the choice of words Brooks has given to Martyn to describe Dean are far from flattering. Dean West is 18 and works in the local 'Gadget Shop'; Martyn's detailed and disparaging description begins:

He was an idiot. Ponytail, long fingernails, bad skin. His face was all the same colour – lips, cheeks, eyes and nose – all rotten and white. He rode a motorbike and liked to think he was some kind of biker, but he wasn't. He was just a pale white idiot (p. 21).

Martyn continues: '...pale face ugly and even whiter than usual... flicking his ponytail from side to side like a cow flicking at flies with its tail...' The bovine reference to cows supports Martyn's judgement of Dean as an 'idiot'.

Already, as reader, hostile thoughts towards Dean have been seeded and when he later addresses Martyn and uses permutations of the abhorrent nicknames Martyn so dislikes, this hostility is made concrete: '...the pigman. At last we finally meet...' (p. 22). He continues, rather unimaginatively in the vein of someone 'idiotic', to address Martyn variously as: 'Pigman', 'Piggy' and 'Pig'. The rapport we have with Martyn's character inevitably leads the reader to resent Dean and question the antagonist's ingenuity.

The character of Alex is less forthcoming in her views of Dean and this creates intrigue on the part of the reader. When pressed by Martyn to explain her association with Dean, Alex becomes angry: 'How the hell would you know what he's like! You've only met him *once*. Christ!' (p. 30). From this we can only assume that the character must have some hidden appeal, if only to Alex. Perhaps it is to do with Dean having all the trappings of an adult's life: the motorbike, the flat and the job. For a girl on the cusp of adulthood these could be alluring factors.

In the Chapter 'Thursday', in which Dean prepares to blackmail Martyn over the £30,000 with his tape-recording of the conversation Alex and Martyn had in the wake of the death, his actions and words begin with a confident conviction to extract the money from Martyn. When he reveals how his machination came to be, with the planting of the bug in Alex's bag, his smile is 'self-satisfied' (p. 66) and yet this chapter also reveals that Dean is fallible; when Martyn accedes to Dean's demand to see the body, the omniscient narrator reveals that 'The corner of his mouth twitched as he spoke, the tiniest of tics, and his left eyelid fluttered in reaction' (p. 67). These physical manifestations suggest that Dean is not the strong man he tries to portray and, faced with seeing a dead body, perhaps for the first time, anxiety manifests itself.

Having viewed the body, it is significant that Brooks has the character of Dean remove himself from the room to splash cold water over his face in the kitchen – this suggests that he has been upset or repulsed by the cadaver and literally wants to wash the image away. Rather than evoking empathy in the reader this steers the reader towards feelings of contempt in the face of Dean's plans; whilst Martyn may have had dislike or even hate for his father, it remains the case that he is also bereaved and in a terrible predicament.

This contempt is solidified on page 67 when the character Alex addresses Dean saying: 'It's none of your business, Dean, you don't *own* me.' To which Dean retorts (tapping the tape recorder): 'I do now'. From a female perspective we translate this as misogyny (hatred, dislike or mistrust of women); the character appears to have taken ownership of Alex as if she were a mere chattel or personal belonging and later, in the chapter 'Monday', the character's misogynistic nature becomes solidified as Brooks chooses to suggest that Dean appreciates Alex in a singularly sexual nature: addressing Martyn, Dean says: "She's too much for you, I know that. Too much of a woman, know what I mean?...I'd stick to someone your own age if I were you. Snogging behind the bike sheds, that kind of stuff. *Kid's* stuff. Alex, she's something else.' He winked. 'She'd wear you out." This insinuation further alienates the character of Dean from any female readers.

When the balance of power shifts from Dean to Martyn, Martyn having orchestrated the means to implicate Dean in his father's death, the author employs the word 'Baby' to highlight the antagonist's weakness:

*He was nothing. Less than nothing, now. Beaten, lost, humiliated, he sat there like a **baby** – a six-foot-tall **baby** dressed in black leather. Helpless, clueless, weak, white and flabby. A gentle breeze would have blown him over. I reached over and took the tape from his hand. Candy from a **baby*** (p. 163).

Martyn's responds to Dean's death on page 191 by questioning his own feelings: 'So why did I feel so bad about Alex killing him? Why did it frighten me? What made it so *wrong?..*', before revealing: '...something gripped me that night, and whatever it was it turned me inside out?' suggests that the antagonist feels the death was needless, which it clearly was. Finally, with Brooks' choice of the word 'baby', which infantilizes the character together with Martyn's emotional response, the reader is drawn to feelings of pity and sorrow for the character of Dean. Alex's callousness in killing Dean entrench this response.

In effect, as the reader, our response to Dean shifts as the story progresses; at first we trust the first-person narrator and harbour feelings of hostility and dislike. Later the character's fallibility is revealed to us. Finally, as the character needlessly dies at the hands of Alex, we respond with feelings of pity and sorrow.

'Home is home, I suppose. No matter how much you hate it, you still need it. You need whatever you're used to. You need security.'

How does Brooks show Martyn's feelings about his home in the novel?

Written in the first person narrative, Martyn addresses the reader directly; the chatty vernacular he uses invites us to empathise with him and we are party to all his thoughts and feelings. This device ensures that, as reader, Martyn's views on home life are patently clear.

In the first chapter, 'Wednesday', Brooks paints a very bleak picture of home life. We learn that Martyn lives with his drunken and abusive father and that he has adopted the role of a responsible adult. He cleans, disposes of his father's empty beer cans and has taken the initiative to train in first aid: 'So I could tell whether he was dead or just dead drunk.' In this home we discover that Martyn has had his wrist broken by his father when he was younger, and, through the use of repetition on page 24, (permutations of the word 'hate'), his feelings are clear: 'Did I hate him? He was a drunken slob and he treated me like dirt. What do *you* think? Of course I hated him.'

Home life for Martyn clearly involves physical risk, something which Martyn is acutely aware of. On page 31 the protagonist describes the stages of his father's 'drunkeness':

Stage One, the first hour or so after he'd started, he'd make out like he was my best pal...Stage Two was mostly self-pitying misery...Stage Three was incoherence with an unpredictable hint of violence...Stage Four – the final stage – was when he collapsed into a drunken coma.'

Through Martyn's disclosure we learn that the home he shares with his father is therefore an unsafe home, the antithesis of the sanctuary we would normally associate with home life and therefore offering very little of the security Martyn associates with home in the question's quotation.

Martyn's mother left as a consequence of his father's alcoholism but failed to take Martyn with her or maintain contact; Martyn, discovering *The Complete Illustrated Sherlock Homes* for his tenth birthday but not remembering who gave it to him, admits: 'It couldn't have been Mum, she was long since gone' (p. 25). From this we can deduce that Martyn's home, prior to his mother's abandonment, was not enhanced by a strong matriarchal presence, certainly the mother appears to have made no effort to maintain contact with her child. In a sense, Martyn is an orphan, having neither paternal nor maternal support. This portrait of family life is thrown into sharp relief with the factual evidence Brooks provides on page 54; Martyn discovers a tin box full of old photographs, not one of which are of him: 'Most of them were of Dad when he was a young man. In a pub with his mates, red-eyed, raising his glass to the camera; at the beach with a gormless-looking girlfriend....There was none of me. And just one of Mum.' This indicates that Martyn has never been a priority within this family.

The home that Martyn describes is filthy by virtue of his father's laziness and bad habits. Martyn finds this mentally disturbing and ritualistically cleans the house. On page 154 he describes the mess and the impact it has on him:

Back home I tidied up. Without Dad around the place was easy to clean. I used to hate the mess he made. Stuff all over the floor, dirty plates and cups, glasses, bottles, newspapers, cigarette ash...it was a tip. As soon as I'd cleared it all away there'd be more. A never ending supply of rubbish. I couldn't stand it. All that jumble and dirt, it made me so I couldn't think straight. I need to see clean surfaces, flat and uncluttered. I need to see the true shape of things, the lines, the angles. Mess messes me up....

However, Martyn's own bedroom provides a sanctuary from the clutter: 'My room was a palace compared to Dad's. Clean and white and odourless. Everything in its place' (p.82). This is, perhaps, the house's only redeeming feature from Martyn's perspective; a place which doesn't 'mess him up.'

On the house's immediate surroundings the narrator describes everything with similes, metaphors and language of bleakness, death and decay:

This house, this place where I lived, this street, this town; I hated it. Dirty-grey. Dark and cold, everything too close. All the people living in dull acceptance of their misery, their drab surroundings. I hated it (p. 58).

Later he reiterates:

The view from the kitchen window hadn't changed. Grey skies hanging over the tops of houses. Dull triangles decorated with dead chimney pots and television aerials. Right angles. Broken gutters. Ugly white satellite dishes (p. 75).

And again: 'Me, alone in a dirty little house, in a dirty little street, in a dirty little town' (p. 96).

Throughout the story the protagonist generally refers to the home with the much less personal word 'house', which serves to emphasize the fact that he feels no fondness towards home. In addition, Martyn is often placed looking out on the world through the windows of the house, almost as if he is held captive by the building. Generally, he then describes the gloom he can see: 'I stood up and went over to the window. Yellowy bits of cloud had crawled into the sky. It looked like a dirty handkerchief' (p. 58).

In addition, Martyn's home is often described as physically cold: 'Wind-blown sheets of rain were rattling against the window. The room was cold. I was shivering' (p. 39). Brooks employs contrast between warmth and cold to demonstrate Martyn's views on his home compared with Alex's home: 'I watched her cross the road back to her house, her home, her mother, her warm bed...I shut the door. The house was still cold. And quiet' (p. 45). Martyn is plainly aware of the isolation and lack of warmth, physical or familial, that his house provides.

Brooks again employs contrast after Martyn has moved in with Aunty Jean. The frequent descriptions of gloom and death are replaced with life and warmth as Martyn again views the world from a window: 'I could see her through the French windows...Spring sunshine flooded in through the open conservatory doors, a smell of fresh flowers breezed in the air' (p. 216). Later he comments: 'It was a nice garden. A long stretch of well-tended lawn bounded by neat flower beds, shrubs, several young willow trees and a small rockery dotted with frosty-green alpine plants. Nice and quiet. Peaceful' (p. 217). The approving descriptions continue on page 218: 'It was a beautiful day. Cloudless blue skies, willow trees waving gently in a slow breeze, birds singing. A lawn mower droned comfortably in the distance.' Martyn's descriptions of the outside area of the house he shared with his father, by comparison, are evocative of a harsh and hostile place: 'The rain was turning to sleet as I pushed open the back gate and shuffled down the alleyway that led to the back of our house, stepping over dog turds and squashed cigarette ends and bin-liners full of empty beer cans' (p. 23). The contrasting descriptions demonstrate that the protagonist is far happier in his new home and in his new pleasant surroundings.

Martyn's newly-found contentment and sense of belonging are confirmed on page 216 when he takes ownership of his new home: 'We were in the conservatory at Aunty Jean's house. My house.'

'You told me once that badness is relative thing – you said something is only wrong if you think it's wrong.'

How bad do you think Alex is and how does Brooks present her in the novel?

Brooks presents Alex through Martyn's eyes and voice as he chooses to tell the story in the first person, so how we see Alex and how bad she is depends to a large extent on the way Martyn sees her. At the very end of the novel when Martyn receives a letter from Alex (who is in America pursuing her dream of becoming an actress), he reacts with tolerance and equanimity to the news – despite the fact that she has stolen £30,000 from him and betrayed all the trust he showed in her.

Alex, whose full name we only discover in the 'Epilogue' is Alexandra Freeman, is an enigmatic character. From one point of view she is completely bad – she cuts the brake cables on her boyfriend's bike and he dies in a collision with a bus, and she steals the £30,000 that belongs to Martyn. However, our view of Alex is filtered and influenced by Martyn's narration, and, while it can be argued that Alex's role in Dean's murder disgusts him, in the 'Epilogue', when we receives a letter from Alex – who is in California trying to break into acting, Martyn reacts with calm equanimity: his affection for Alex almost makes him tolerant of her crime of theft and he seems to forgive her.

For most of the novel Alex is presented as unequivocally good. She is Martyn's best friend and her creation allows Brooks to write dialogue between the two of them – she is Martyn's confidante and, when she visits on the night that his father dies, Martyn has no hesitation in telling her exactly what has happened. In the few days that follow Alex helps Martyn move his father's corpse from the living room to the bed – so that they can trick Aunty Jean into believing that her brother is alive. She handles the corpse, applies make up to Dad's face and even makes a recording of him breathing and wheezing – showing off her acting skills and her ability to imitate voices. She appears genuinely upset when Dean presents his blackmail threat to Martyn and demands that he hand over the £30,000 to him or he will reveal all to the police. On Saturday she borrows her mother's car so that she and Martyn can dispose of the corpse in the quarry – and all this, it seems to Martyn, is done for him and for the sake of their friendship.

The reader shares Martyn's faith in Alex simply because we have no other point of view, no other option – and because Brooks has chosen to write the novel in the first person we assume, as Martyn does, that Alex does everything for the sake of her friendship with him. However, doubts start to enter Martyn's mind on Sunday evening when Alex clearly lies to him about where she was that morning: she says she was out with her mother, but Martyn knows that is a lie because he has spoken with her mother on Sunday morning. As the rest of the novel unfolds, Martyn realizes that Alex, with the connivance of her mother, has stolen the money and fled to America with his money.

Although Martyn's gradual realization of the truth adds to the tension, interest and excitement of the novel, Brooks has in a way prepared us for her betrayal by his presentation of Alex: it is only when we look back at the whole novel can we see the truth. For example, every time she and Martyn part, Martyn watches her but 'She didn't look back'; what might see like a trivial detail becomes (because Brooks repeats it whenever she leaves) a leitmotif for Alex's ability to move on with her life and her lack of loyalty or any sense of obligation to the past and to those who considered her a friend. In the same way, her ability to act is established by Brooks in the first chapter and is frequently reinforced. Therefore, we have to ask ourselves whether Alex is simply acting when she seems so upset by Dean's clumsy attempt to blackmail Martyn. On pages 68 and 69 we are told that 'Alex had been crying. She was sitting at the kitchen table pulling a paper tissue to pieces' – but perhaps she is acting.

Perhaps the way she is presented on Monday – on her return from Dean's flat Martyn notices that 'She was like someone else' (p. 166) - is not, as Martyn assumes, a reaction to all the stress of the previous few days, but actually a sense of regret and guilt at what she and her mother plan to do the next day and a reaction to the fact that she knows she will never see Martyn again. Martyn assumes she is suffering from 'Shock, probably. That's all it is. That's all it is. A bit of a shock' (p. 166). Ironically Martyn may be right – but the shock she is feeling is not due to her visit to Dean's flat, but to her murder of Dean and to her imminent betrayal of Martyn. Later in the chapter she is very evasive when Martyn presses her to discuss their plans for what to do with the money which they will get on the Tuesday morning, Christmas Eve. In retrospect we can see that she is evasive because she knows that she and her mother intend to steal Martyn's money on the following morning.

Martyn's narrative encourages the reader to be calm and tolerant in the face of Alex's behavior, but in absolute terms Alex is a bad person: she takes actions which lead to the death of Dean and she steals Martyn's money. Martyn did once say that 'something is only wrong if you think it's wrong', but although he is calm when he receives Alex's letter, we should not forget his reaction at the police station when he realized Alex had murdered Dean – he vomited spontaneously and copiously, suggesting that at a deep level Martyn believes that a crime such as murder is always wrong. He says himself on page 191 of Alex's killing of Dean – ''What made it so wrong?' However, Martyn's lingering affection for Alex enables him to hide from the truth that Alex is a bad person and to protect her from the police in 'Epilogue'. Alex is a thief and a murderer without a conscience.

How do you respond to Martyn in the novel?

You should write about:

- **What you think about Martyn from what he says and does**

- **The methods Brooks uses to present Martyn**

The book begins in the first person narrative; Martyn immediately disclosing that his mother is absent from his life and describing how circumstances beyond his control have made him the object of ridicule. Namely the spelling of his given name with a 'y' rather, than an 'i' and his surname: 'Pig'. He says of this: 'My name made my life unbearable. Why did I have to put up with it? The startled looks, the sneers and sniggers...' (p. 7) The character goes on to describe the hurtful name-calling: 'Porky, Piggy, Pigman, Oink, Bacon, Stinky, Snorter, Porker, Grunt...' (p. 8). The combined effect of the first person narrative and the forthright admission of the character's pain elicit feelings of sympathy from the reader.

The protagonist then describes his home life with his ill-educated, alcoholic, idle and abusive father. The author chooses to apply correct English for Martyn's narrative but highlights, via Martyn's quotations, the poor English of his father: "Bloody emviroment this, emviroment that...if anyone wants to use my empty bottles again they'll have to pay for 'em...What's the emviroment ever done for me?" (p. 9). The contrast, again, elicits feelings of sympathy displaying the conflict of intellect, personality and lifestyle between father and son. Brooks' repetition of permutations of the word 'hate' in association with Martyn's father cement these feelings:

Did I hate him? He was a drunken slob and he treated me like dirt...of course I hated him. You would have hated him, too...Yeah, I hated him. I hated every inch of him... I hated his beery guts... (p. 24)

They way in which the character directly addresses the reader and even asks questions of the reader gives the protagonist a real sense of authenticity: 'I know what you're thinking. Why didn't I ring 999, call out the emergency services?...I don't know. I just didn't. All right?' (p. 38). It feels as if Martyn is a friend making a confession.

The author uses alliteration and free association to comic effect, which suggests that Martyn is a daydreamer with a creative mind, something which sustains a rapport between character and reader throughout the book and also provides a break from the gloom of the subject matter and surroundings: 'Snow. Snowball. Snowdrop. Drop of snow. Snowgoose. That's no goose, that's my wife. Snowshoe. Bless you...' (p. 106) and 'Molasses? What *are* molasses? Mole asses. Mole arses. A boat full of moles' arses' (p. 103).

Throughout the book Martyn is portrayed as an isolated observer on a grey and murky world. Brooks repeatedly uses the device of a window to highlight Martyn's isolation as the character looks out on his forlorn surroundings: 'I opened the bedroom curtains and gazed out at the colours of the day. Grey, brown. Brown, grey. Black. Dead green...Dead green spikes drooped with the weight of frost' (p. 99); 'I watched through the window as the sun rose slowly and nudged away the dead cold blackness of the night. It wasn't much to see, the birth of another grey day...' (p. 49). Despite the fact we know that Martyn's circumstances are quite bleak, having accidently killed his father, the repeatedly dreary descriptions of his surroundings create a sense of irritation, this combined with the fact that the character needlessly covers up his father's death. As a reader, or spectator – we develop a growing irritation with the character – his negativity and his inaction after the death of his father.

The character's descriptions of other characters in the book suggest that Martyn is quite intolerant of others and would rather see the negative side of people. At times his descriptions can be cruel, and this adds to the sense of frustration and makes us question Martyn's sense of fairness. Aunty Jean is described variously as: 'a blue-haired, bow-legged dragon lady' (p. 91); 'She smelled of lemon and bleach and awful old-woman perfume' (p. 87); 'Her hair sat on top her head like a blue Brillo pad...' (p. 86). However, by the end of the novel we know that Aunty Jean has Martyn's best interests at heart. Similarly, Sergeant Finlay is described as: 'sad-faced, about thirty, he looked a bit dim...' (p. 182). Martyn applies an equally cruel description to the social worker: 'He was a weedy-looking young man with short ginger hair and short ginger moustache that was hardly worth the bother of growing... he looked like a bell-ringer... his voice was too boring to listen to...' (p. 201). The character's collective mistrust of adults, as demonstrated via Brooks' descriptions, evokes a real sense of misguided negativity which serves to frustrate the reader who is party to the knowledge that none of these characters harbour any malice towards Martyn.

Do you think that *Martyn Pig* is an exciting novel?

Write about:

- **What makes you think it is an exciting novel, or not**

- **The methods the writer uses to make you respond the way you do.**

Martyn Pig is an exciting novel and Brooks structures the novel carefully so that every chapter, until the very end of the novel, ends with an unresolved question which helps maintain tension and excitement for the reader. Ironically, given Martyn's interest in detective fiction and murder mysteries, there is little excitement generated by Dad's death: the cover of the novel tells us that he is going to die, and Martyn is completely open about his father's accidental death. The excitement is generated by wondering whether and how Martyn will succeed in covering up the facts of Dad's death, so that he avoids any blame for it. Dean's attempt to blackmail Martyn is a further complication that Brooks adds to the plot which produces excitement and tension as the reader waits expectantly to see if Martyn can deal effectively with Dean and his threats.

As soon as Martyn has chosen not to contact the emergency services when his father dies he is left with a problem: how to dispose of the body and, before that, how to convince his Aunty Jean that her brother is alive. The body's disposal has to wait until Saturday, because Alex's Mum's car is being repaired and in any case Aunty Jean's visit is scheduled for Friday. Brooks adds to Martyn's problems and, therefore, to the excitement of the novel by adding Dean's threat to blackmail Martyn – which occurs on Thursday: Dean expects to receive the money on Monday. These three events – and the question of whether or not they will pass successfully - generate excitement: Friday's visit of Aunty Jean, the disposal of the Dad's corpse on Saturday, and Martyn's confrontation with Dean on Monday, and keep the reader in a state of tension. With Dean we know that Martyn has a plan because he tells Alex and the reader so on page 72, but Brooks is careful not to divulge the plan to the readers so our excitement and our anticipation of Martyn's meeting with Dean on Monday is increased. In fact, these three potential problems pass without incident: Aunty Jean is convinced her brother is alive; Alex and Martyn dispose of the body without any problems; Dean's threat is dealt with effectively. However, we might note that Martyn achieves all this only with the help of Alex: without her, he could not have carried out any of his plans. Brooks cleverly adds a hint to increase our unease on Sunday evening: Alex lies to Martyn about where she had been that morning – although the significance of that lie is not made clear until Tuesday.

However, it could be argued that the real excitement and tension enter the plot in the chapters 'Tuesday' and 'Christmas Day' when Martyn is not sure where Alex is and when his careful planning of the events surrounding the disposal of his Dad's body and standing up to Dean starts go awry. 'Tuesday' is an especially exciting chapter, because, through Brooks' use of the first person narrator, Martyn does not know where Alex is or what she is doing. In the course of the chapter Brooks allows Martyn, very slowly, to come to a realization of what must have happened, but it is made exciting because we have access to Martyn's innermost thoughts and because his realization is so slowly arrived at. Martyn has worked out for himself that Alex and her mother have disappeared and stolen his money. He takes so long to come to this conclusion partly because of his feelings towards Alex: he has shown total trust in her and counted her as his only friend, so it is hard for the character to face up to the truth of the fact that she has betrayed him. There is worse to come: towards the end of the chapter, at night, the police call on Martyn, wanting to ask him questions. They reveal that Dean has been killed in a road accident when his motorbike crashed into a bus – the accident occurred because someone had cut the brake cables on his motorbike. All this is possible because Brooks has chosen to tell the story from Martyn's point of view in a first-person narrative, and Martyn has no idea that Alex will betray him.

At this stage the excitement is two-fold. On the one hand, the involvement of the police makes us tense because we don't know what they might accuse Martyn of doing – although in the event Martyn handles their questions well both in this chapter and on 'Christmas Day' when they carry out a longer interrogation. The other source of excitement comes from Martyn's racing thoughts trying to make sense of events. In his room at the police station he finally comes to the conclusion that Alex must have cut Dean's brake cables and that she has murdered Dean. Not only have she and her mother stolen Martyn's money, they have also conspired to murder Alex's boyfriend. Martyn's reaction is telling: 'my stomach heaved and the next thing I knew I was kneeling in front of the toilet bowl being sicker than I'd ever thought possible' (p. 191). The chapter ends tensely too, because at this stage Martyn does not know whether Alex has left clues which will help to implicate him or Dean in the murder of his father. We have to wait until the next chapter to realize that the evidence Alex has planted at Dean's flat is designed to make the police link Dean with Dad's death. Martyn is released from police custody and the novel – apart from 'Epilogue' – is over.

Martyn Pig is an exciting novel: in the first part we feel tension over whether Martyn can dispose of his father's body and survive the interventions of Aunty Jean and Dean. The real excitement occurs, ironically, when Martyn has completed these tasks successfully and is faced with the uncertainty over where Alex is and what she has done. At this point the novel resembles the detective fiction that Martyn loves so much and, as readers, we are able to look back and see the clues or hints that, in retrospect, show us Alex was planning to betray Martyn all along.

How does Brooks present Martyn's visit to the beach and how is this visit important to the novel as a whole?

Brooks establishes Martyn's incentive for the beach visit as a need to 'get some fresh air into my lungs, air that wasn't stained with the musk of stale death.' (p.100) Saturday's beach trip probably represents the protagonist's lowest point and, as he journeys to his destination, the narrative is full of pessimistic and cynical description, the fields are 'dead-looking' (p.102), whilst there are 'false barns selling fruit and veg and false fresh eggs', similarly, signs spotted en-route are described as 'meaningless'. The language suggests a slide into a depressive state.

The contemplation of death is a predominant theme in this particular extract. Brooks draws heavily on permutations of the word 'death' throughout the beach scene: 'half dead dog'; 'the wind had died (p.104); 'carcass of a dead porpoise' (p.105) before examining Martyn's own feelings on morbidity: 'If I sit here long enough, I thought, I'll die. I'll freeze to death...Would that be so bad? I wondered. Would it hurt?' (p.107).

Brooks explores in the beach extract Martyn's relationship with the concept of home and, as with the book in its entirety, the protagonist's emotions continue to oscillate wildly: the author writes: 'It felt strange being out of the house. Exciting, but a little scary too. I wasn't used to it. My world consisted of my house, the street, school and the occasional trip to town.' (p.102). The protagonist appears to relish the isolation the beach affords: 'The exciting part about it was that no one knew where I was. No one. Not a soul.' (p. 102) However, as the ethereal scene morphs into the grotesque, with the vision of Alex and its metamorphosis into his drunken father, Martyn's attitude changes. This is significant because it is the precursor to Martyn's epiphany at the end of the beach extract in which he concludes that: 'Home is home, I suppose. No matter how much you hate it, you still need it. You need whatever you're used to. You need security.' (p. 112)

The beach scene is perhaps the most ethereal of all the chapters and suggests to the reader that the protagonist is losing his sense of reality. Brooks employs several devices to achieve this. Firstly, he employs oxymorons to create ambiguity describing the sky as a: 'white darkness' (p.105) and snowflakes are presented as 'silent and serene – menacing.' Also, as with a dream, the passage of time is warped: 'Time seemed to have disappeared. Not stopped or slowed down, just disappeared.' (p. 106) Martyn, on returning home, discovers that it is just five past two: 'I couldn't believe it. I thought I'd been gone for ages.' (p. 111). At the end of the vision the character asks: 'Was that really Alex? Was it a dream? Was it real?' (p.109). In addition Brooks uses passages of free association, which heighten the sense of the surreal: 'Sea. The sea. Salt water. Brine. Brian. Call me Brian. Destiny. Sea. Adriatic Sea. South China Sea. Irish Sea. Red Sea. The Dead Sea. The dead see…' (p.107). We witness the protagonist emotionally unravelling with thoughts departed from reality: 'It did happen though. I'm sure it did. Believe it. Or dont'. (p. 111).

We learn that the beach is really an island, a place Martyn describes as '…empty. Cold, big, wide open and deserted.' (p.101). The geographical landscape, together with Martyn's self-deprecatory description of himself: 'I imagine myself as a tiny black dot, a blind particle crawling through the snow and sand. An insect. Going nowhere. Alone. Indeterminate, immeasurable and shapeless. Nothing much at all.' (p.105), elicit feelings of pity in the reader; Martyn is isolated, a tiny thing on an island expanse. The first person narrative contributes to the reader's empathy with direct access into the character's inner-most thoughts, and this effectively creates a deepening rapport between reader and character for the remaining chapters.

Brooks uses different places in *Martyn Pig*. Choose two of these places and write about them.

You should write about:

- ## what happens in each place

- ## why both places are important.

The methods Brooks uses to present these places.

Places are very important in *Martyn Pig* and Brooks presents them as important to his central character, Martyn, because he uses Martyn to describe certain places at length – mainly through sight and sound – and Martyn is presents by Brooks as being very aware of his surroundings – places often shape or reflect Martyn's mood.

Dad's bedroom is presented as the complete antithesis of Martyn's and his father's bedroom represents all the things Martyn dislikes. He admits that he has not even entered his Dad's bedroom for years – since his mother left the house. What Martyn does not like about his Dad's room is that is untidy and dirty. Brooks conveys this through visual descriptions and occasionally mentioning smells as well:

Dad's room was a heap. Curls of wallpaper peeled from the walls revealing old layers of sick-yellow paint. Magazines littered the floor....the bed was unmade and smelled unwashed. Bits of broken biscuits and breadcrumbs lay scattered beneath the duvet…. (p. 52)

It is clear that Dad, who took no pride in his personal appearance, also took no pride in the up-keep or general cleanliness of his own room. On the bedside table there are 'an ashtray and a pint glass half-filled with dusty water' (p. 52). Martyn goes on to comment and observe:

The ashtray stank….A trail of discarded clothes led from the bed to the wardrobe – pants, socks, a vest, crumpled trousers and shirts. A polystyrene burger box lay half-hidden beneath a dirty vest. Two halves of a burger bun, hard and stale and burgerless, crusty and forgotten. (p. 52).

This is squalid and unhygienic.

By contrast Martyn's room is an oasis of peace and tidiness in the squalor of his home. He tells us that his room used to be crowded with old toys and books but

But I threw most of it out about a year ago. All my old stuff. I just got fed up with it. One Saturday afternoon I got a couple of those big green garden refuse sacks, the extra strong ones, and piled everything I didn't want any more into them. Then I lugged the sacks down to the council tip and chucked them in a skip. (pp. 144 – 145)

The result is that now his room is 'bare and empty, which is just the way I like it….No pictures, no posters, no ornaments. Nice and clean. Functional' (p. 145). We might note that this is the complete opposite of his father's room. Martyn's desire for order and neatness is symbolized by his bedroom.

Dad's room and Martyn's room are typical of the places that Martyn likes or dislikes in the whole novel. Martyn's house is presented as typical of the area in which he lives – a working class area of a small English town. That is why the snow fall on Sunday morning is so welcome to Martyn. It transforms the area he lives in:

The street lay covered in snow. Crispy and white, - cars, walls, the road, the

pavement. All the muck and the dirt was hidden beneath a pure white blanket of snow. (p. 137)

The places that Martyn liked and feels comfortable in are clean, tidy and functional – it always helps if they are quiet and there are no discordant sounds. He writes on page 155, 'Mess messes me up', and this is true of life as well as his home – when he has no contact from Alex on Tuesday, his mind races feverishly trying to work out what has happened, to bring tidiness to events which have spiralled out of control. On 'Christmas Eve' when he is taken to the police station for questioning about Dean's death, Martyn has the calmness to notice that:

The police station was clean and brightly lit. A low, pale brick building at the edge of town, it was surrounded by sparse lawns and smooth sloping driveways. A calming place. It was quiet. An oasis in a desert of smell-town noise. (p. 188)

It makes sense for Martyn to have these feelings since the house he has grown up in and the area he lives in are dull, dirty and squalid. At the very end of the novel, despite his fears of being sent to live with Aunty Jean, he seems happy to be there as 'Aunty Jean was spring-cleaning… polishing like a mad thing in the front room, stooped over the dining table with her sleeves rolled up, her polishing arm working pumping away like a piston' (p. 216). One major reason for his contentment at Aunty Jean's is the cleanliness and order which is such a contrast to his old home with Dad.

How does Brooks present ideas about control or lack of control in *Martyn Pig*?

Martyn hardly ever uses the word 'control' in the novel, but nonetheless it is an important underlying concept, as is its opposite – a lack of control – and these ideas underpin Martyn's character, how Brooks presents him and his way of looking at life, and even his mood and state of mind.

Martyn likes to be in control, yet at the start of the novel he has no control over his own life: he is bullied by his father and does anything and everything his father wants him to – with the threat of verbal abuse and physical violence always lurking in the back ground. Even Martyn's favourite pastime – reading detective stories – evinces a desire for control, since in almost all detective stories the main character (a leading detective), from a mass of evidence, false trails and genuine clues, solves the case and brings a murderer to justice and, in doing so, restores a sense of control to the fictional world of the novel. In one sense, by choosing to use Martyn as the first-person narrator of the novel, Brooks gives Martyn the illusion of control. Certainly as we read the novel we know everything that Martyn knows and through his narration we are told his innermost thoughts – but just as Brooks controls what Martyn tells us, he also controls what Martyn knows, and it turns out that Martyn is not in control of the events that are triggered by his Dad's death.

After his father's accidental death, Martyn appears to be in full control of events. He plans the disposal of the body; he manages to convince his Aunty Jean that his father, her brother, is alive when she comes to visit; even when faced with Dean's attempt to blackmail him, he comes up with a plan that implicates Dean in the murder of Martyn's Dad. In terms of the plot and its sequence, Martyn is in control, or thinks he is until Dean's visit to his house on Monday – a visit that coincides with Alex planting more evidence of Dean's involvement with Martyn's father's death at Dean's flat. Again, because of the first-person narration, we share Martyn's belief that he is in control.

However, it is notable that the disposal of Dad's body and the implication of Dean in his 'murder' could not have been achieved without Alex: they use her mother's car to move the body to the quarry; she helps Martyn move Dad's body from the living room upstairs to his bedroom where Aunty Jean sees him; she applies make up to Dad to make him look alive and makes a recording pretending to be Dad, breathing and wheezing to convince Aunty Jean that her brother is alive; because she has a key to Dean's flat, she is able to bring some of his hairs and discarded cigarette butts which are then planted in the sleeping bag with Dad's body before Alex and Martyn throw it in the gravel pit; she also makes use of her access to Dean's flat on Monday while Dean is at Martyn's house, by planting some of the solicitor's letters about the £30,000 and some pieces of paper on which Martyn had demonstrated his ability to forge his father's signature. Without Alex, Martyn's plans could not have been accomplished – but the apparent success of his plans gives Martyn and the reader the illusion that he is in control.

However, there is a further twist that Brooks is able to introduce because he has chosen to use Martyn as a first-person narrator. Unknown to Martyn and the reader, Alex has been plotting to steal his money and also dispose of Dean – which she accomplishes after she has cut the brake cables on his motorbike and he dies in an accident with a bus. All the time Martyn thought he was in control of the situation, manipulating events and evidence to frame Dean for his father's murder. However, unknown to Martyn and to the reader, Alex is planning to betray him and steal his money, while ensuring that Dean is framed for Martyn's father's death.

The question of control or lack of control is also intimately linked with the way Martyn reacts to physical places and to people. His Dad, we might argue, demonstrates no control over himself – he is a slave to his addiction to alcohol and to cigarettes – and exercises little control over the house he shares with Martyn. By contrast, Martyn's room is very neat and tidy, showing Martyn's desire for control of the environment he lives in. Martyn's cleaning of the house after his Dad's death symbolizes Martyn regaining control of the house. One of the things that makes living with his Aunty Jean bearable for Martyn is the tidiness and neatness of her house and garden: 'a long stretch of well-tended lawn bounded by neat flower beds, shrubs, several young willow trees and a small rockery dotted with frosty-green alpine plants. Nice and quiet. Peaceful' (p. 217). As with dirt and untidiness, Martyn, throughout the novel, has shown a strong preference for places which are quiet and he reacts badly to noisy, discordant places – where he cannot control what he hears: we might remember his panic attack in The Bargain Bin in the opening chapter where the uncontrolled noise around him caused him great anxiety.

In addition, the most tense moments in the novel are in the police station where Martyn slowly and fully works out what Alex and her mother have done, and he realizes he has lost control of events that he thought he was shaping.

Therefore, it can be seen in his reading habits, in his predilection for order and peace, and his attempts to control the events that follow from his Dad's death, the central character and narrator likes control and is always made uncomfortable or ill-at-ease by a lack of control. In another sense, Martyn has no control over his fate: he had predicted that he would end up living with Aunty Jean – and he does! The brief dream of the £30,000 allows him to have fantasies which put him in control of his life. By the same token, Brooks has controlled the plot of *Martyn Pig* so adroitly that right up to the end of the novel there are twists and turns reminiscent of a detective novel.

The ending of *Martyn Pig* may come as a surprise to the reader.

What do you find surprising (or not) about the ending, and how does Brooks prepare the reader for this ending in the rest of the novel?

The novel comes to its physical ending in the 'Epilogue' and contains few surprises. Martyn is living with his Aunty Jean, something he had predicted all along, telling Alex on page 42 that it was inevitable. There is a minor surprise in his discovery that, like his father, Aunty Jean too likes alcohol. Martyn describes his father's funeral in his usual cynical and bitter way: The police too have visited Martyn in an effort to solve the mystery of his father's death. Breece has made some progress and discovered that Martyn knew Alex. On page 217 Breece asks Martyn, 'How well did you know Alexandra Freeman?' and Martyn is momentarily perplexed: 'I nearly choked on my tea' (p. 217). But by a series of lies and half-truths, Martyn is able to deflect Breece's interest in Alex – prior to this Martyn has been careful not to mention her at all. He is clearly protecting her from the consequences of her murderous act of cutting the brake cables on Dean's motorbike, while still protecting himself from his accidental part in Dad's death.

The novel ends with the arrival of a letter from Alex who is now in California with her mother, pursuing a career in acting – in one sense, this is not surprising: Alex had admitted her ambition was to be an actress and had demonstrated her ability to act when she mimicked Dad's voice and made the recording of him breathing and mumbling for Aunty Jean's visit. In another sense, Alex has been acting with Martyn for much, if not all, of the novel. Because of the first-person narration, we do not know exactly when Alex began to plan to steal Martyn's money, but it may have been as soon as she heard about it. Brooks prepares us for these aspects of the 'Epilogue' by making clear through the novel Martyn's affection for Alex, and by making it clear that he prefers tidiness and order to dirt and chaos: we are not surprised that he seems to like Aunty Jean's house and garden.

Although Alex's letter brings closure to the novel, it is not surprising in itself. What is more surprising in the 'Epilogue' as a whole, is, firstly, that Martyn quite likes living with his Aunty Jean –the house is in a more wealthy part of town and it is clean and has an immaculate garden – and, secondly, that Martyn reacts so calmly to Alex's letter. Perhaps his lingering affection for her is the reason for his phlegmatic response; he may also have a sneaking admiration for the cunning way she out-planned him during the events of the novel. Of course, Martyn has known for a long time that Alex stole his money and that either Alex or her mother went to the bank, disguised as his father, to withdraw the cash – where she goes and what she does with it is irrelevant. He has long ago worked out that she betrayed him.

Of course, the main narrative ended on Christmas Day the year before – and that really did come as a surprise. It reaches its climax when Martyn, working things out in his head, realizes that Alex has not only stolen his money but murdered her supposed boyfriend, Dean and in fact, unknown to Martyn, she has really been in control of events. This realization prompts a visceral response from Martyn: 'my stomach heaved and the next thing I knew I was kneeling in front of the toilet being sicker than I'd ever thought possible' (p. 191). This is the real surprise towards the end of the novel and it acts exactly like the twist at the end of detective fiction – where the murderer is revealed, and the murderer is Alex.

Brooks prepares us for this ending as early as Sunday – when Martyn eventually speaks to Alex on the phone he realizes she has lied to him. On Monday the plan to prevent Dean's blackmail of Martyn works well, but, ominously, at the end of that chapter when Alex leaves his house, without explanation, Martyn writes, 'That was the last time I ever saw her' (p. 173). Brooks prepares us in other ways through prolepsis: in retrospect, the fact that Alex – whenever she leaves Martyn – 'never looked back' and this can be seen as symbolic – perhaps of her lack of real feelings for Martyn or perhaps conveying the idea that she knows that her future lies elsewhere.

In conclusion, there is little surprising in the 'Epilogue': Martyn is in a safe, clean place and relatively happy; Alex's letter brings closure, but is hardly an earth-shattering surprise. The real twist and the really surprising event is the revelation that Alex is a murderer.

'Whatever I do, I'll still end up at Aunty Jean's.'

What do you think is Aunty Jean's importance in the novel and how does Brooks present her?

Aunty Jean is first introduced to the book by her brother, Billy – Martyn's father, in the initial chapter: 'That bloody woman's coming Friday' (p.10). While Billy doesn't expand on the reasoning behind his description of Aunty Jean, the narrator, in the form of Martyn, takes over, describing Aunty Jean variously as:

A terrible woman. Think of the worst person you know, then double it...I can hardly bear to describe her...Furious...Mad, ugly and furious...An angular woman, cold and hard...her eyes... have as much warmth as two depthless pools. Her mouth is thin and pillar-box red, like something drawn by a disturbed child... (p. 10)

Significantly, Billy and Martyn Pig's views of Aunty Jean, are alike and within the book this represents an anomaly. Effectively, their attitudes towards Aunty Jean coincide making Aunty Jean the one thing that they can agree on. Martyn reveals that his father: '...detested her. Hated her. He was scared stiff of the woman' (p. 10-11). On page 85 the narrator's description of the door bell ringing demonstrates that Martyn also harbours this fear: 'I could tell it was Aunty Jean by the tone of the bell. It sounded terrified' (p. 85). The very fact that the prospect of living at Aunty Jean's house is pivotal to Martyn's decision not to involve the police supports this fear.

We learn that after Billy's wife left, Aunty Jean had sought custody of Martyn. Of this the narrator reveals that:

She wanted me to live with her, not with Dad. God knows why, she never liked me...she wasn't going to 'stand by and let him ruin an innocent young boy's life too.' Which was all a load of rubbish. She didn't give a hoot for my innocent life, she just wanted to kick Dad while he was down... (p. 11)

It is clear from this that our narrator surmises that Aunty Jean's motives for wanting to take him in are not based upon empathy or philanthropy, merely a desire to inflict hardship and pain on Martyn's Dad. Later, when the prospect of living with Aunty Jean again emerges, the narrator responds with: 'Christ! I can't live with her, I can't *stand* that woman. She's worse than Dad' (p. 43). However, as the book evolves, as readers, we begin to re-examine Aunty Jean's motives and question the first person narrative. When Brooks has her enquire as to Martyn's wellbeing and how he is doing at school, her persistence in the face of his evasiveness begins to reveal a rather more concerned relative. On page 87 she enquires: "'Now then, Martyn," she said in her very serious voice, "I want you to tell me the truth."', she continues: "How *are* you?' she breathed, *'Really.'* The effect of this is that the author creates a tension between the protagonist's and reader's position on Aunty Jean's involvement; while Martyn continues to detest his Aunt and question her motives, the reader becomes more convinced that Aunty Jean's intentions are without malice. In essence, the reliability of the narrator becomes diminished. Finally, the death of Dad serves to destroy the assertion that Aunty Jean's motives are based upon the desire to hurt Dad who is clearly no longer around to be hurt.

We know that 'home' is an important thing to Martyn, whatever the circumstances: 'Home is home, I suppose. No matter how much you hate it, you still need security. You need whatever you're used to...' (p.112). To support this, throughout the book, the character is often seen inside looking out on the world and when he joins Aunty Jean at her home this behaviour appears to remain unchanged: '...she always wants to know where I'm going, where I've been... Not that it really matters, I hardly ever go anywhere' (p. 212). Despite the protagonist's cruel descriptions of Aunty Jean, at the end of the book she facilitates the security which the character so clearly craves and evidently has his best interests at heart, of which Brooks writes:

There's plenty of Aunty's crap to deal with. She's forever trying to educate me... boring little parties, nice people, manners, hobbies... 'Get yourself a hobby, Martyn, for goodness sake – rambling, bird-watching, something healthy...' (p. 212).

Having moved in with Aunty Jean, Brooks' description of Martyn's immediate surroundings are transformed, the dismal descriptions of cloud and rain peppered throughout the book (eg. 'I watched through the window as the sun rose slowly and nudged away the dead cold blackness of the night. It wasn't much to see, the birth of another grey day...' (p. 49)) give way to much more uplifting narrative: 'I could see through the French windows...spring sunshine flooded in...a smell of fresh flowers breezed in the air...it was a beautiful day' (p. 216 and 218). These markedly different descriptions, pre- and post-living at Aunty Jean's, suggest that Aunty Jean, ironically, represents Martyn's ultimate saviour.

Furthermore, at the end of the book, now living with Aunty Jean, the character of Martyn is presented as a much more relaxed boy, far slower to judge. On page 95, having endured the torment of an alcoholic and brutal father, the narrator reveals that: 'Alcohol. It sucks the life out of a face and replaces it with its own dumb shine of inanity. It's up to you. If you want to lose yourself, have a drink.' Ironically, it transpires in the final pages that Aunty Jean is also an alcoholic: 'But it's alright, I don't really mind. She doesn't get violent or anything, she's more of a maudlin drunk. She just cries a lot. Nice, quiet, drunken tears' (p.213). The character of Aunty Jean introduces a new-found tolerance to the protagonist, who up until now, has perhaps understandably had a blanket mis-trust of his elders and a black-and-white view of the world. Aunty Jean represents the facilitator of acceptance in an imperfect world.

Printed in Great Britain
by Amazon

44686382R00068